Editorial

An American friend wrote to me in response to an article in *Publishers weekly*. It described the changing culture in American publishing, with the currently open-ended strike by part of the staff at HarperCollins's New York Offices in the background. She was remembering her own early experience. 'I cannot imagine working only eight hours a day in publishing. We always attended various daily meetings and frequently could meet print deadlines only by reading manuscripts during some evenings and weekends. The starting salaries and profit margins were indeed low, but book editing and publishing were nonetheless an interesting and sometimes glamorous way to make a living – and it is a career that makes a difference. Of course, the increasingly corporate atmosphere that monitors screen time and keystrokes can get on one's nerves...'

HarperCollins is currently a subsidiary of News Corps which recorded record profits in 2021. It claims that the average salary of a HarperCollins employee is $55,000. The minimum salary is $45,000. 'None of that is an amount you can live on in New York City', said a spokesperson for the strikers. The company asks its employees to come into the Manhattan office at least one day a week – working requirements that have gone beyond 'hybrid'. Strikers do manage regularly to attend the picket lines outside the main offices. They are represented (there must be a story here) by the United Auto Workers' Union. The employers' spokesman declared, 'HarperCollins has agreed to a number of proposals that the UAWU is seeking to include in a new contract. We are disappointed an agreement has not been reached and will continue to negotiate in good faith.'

My friend's experience of publishing did not take for granted the contractual eight (or seven and a half) hour working day as an applicable measure to a job which also saw itself as a vocation, a collaboration with specific writers, booksellers and the reader. It was a vocation that could hardly be more central to the making and dissemination of literature, and of written works with less grand pretensions.

The independent little press publishers and their staffs today must seem an anachronism to the people who debate the merger of Simon and Schuster and Penguin, recently blocked by an American judge on monopoly grounds, and to UAWU negotiators. Their bigger public world reminds us of the eponymous game, publishers gathering up in their skirts whole neighbourhoods of imprints – The Angel Islington, Pentonville Road, Marlborough Street, and (just before the game is over) Park Lane and Mayfair.

CB Books turns fifteen this year and Charles Boyle wrote a brief memoir of his experiences of publishing, from his inheritance of £2,000 from a kindly uncle to his unsubsidised and critically acclaimed, if commercially reluctant, enterprise (see CB editions newsletter 15 November). He has two handsome shelves of books to his credit, most of them unusual and all of them distinctive in presentation and design. Some of them are *poetry*.

To larger publishers, poetry, traditionally Cinderella to the well-heeled ugly sisters of fiction and cookery, can provide an unexpected profit centre. There are big commercial successes – the Rupi Kaur and Amanda Gorman phenomena. Some commercial lists add well-known poetry editors and commission first collections, import American success and resurrect the dead, giving their titles high profile marketing and advertising. Agents are alert to poets, too, in part at least because they occasionally turn in successful prose books. Advances for some kinds of poetry are substantial. Creative writing programmes (run by publishers themselves) encourage poets whose plausibility makes the work of editors more challenging than it once was. Despite these developments, a larger transformation has not yet taken place. Commercially successful poetry books remain exceptions, career poets who actually make a living from royalty earnings are few and far between. Most career poets survive by teaching creative writing and giving public readings. The poetry collection is a passport as well as a glacially slow-selling commodity.

Independent poetry presses are to the main book trade rather as independent booksellers are to Waterstones. They are different less in kind than in culture, concentrating on readership rather than market. This year Arts Council England's National Portfolio Organisations applied for a further three years' funding; once again the forms publishers were required to complete did not mention 'readers': the word 'audience' underlined an inherent bias. The kinds of data clients are expected to gather have to do with attendance at events rather than attendance to printed texts. A careful distance was kept from artistic questions, as though they were peripheral.

PN Review benefits from Arts Council support under the Carcanet Press RFO umbrella. We are grateful for support for a further three years. In that time we will encourage the Council to relearn the word 'reader' as a constituent member of our cultural population, and to recognise that the distinct art forms and each client are different in kind from one another, just as CB Editions in its fifteen years has never once resembled Penguin Books or Hachette – or Bloodaxe, Seren or Carcanet – and yet has produced some literary landmarks. I doubt that Charles Boyle could, even if he wished to, provide a job description for what he does. I doubt that he earns the HarperCollins minimum wage or could bring himself to conform to the conditions of a contracted employee.

Letters to the Editor

Anthony Barnett writes:

I considered writing a full review but I may be out of my depth. I hope this letter will suffice. It is a complaint about style, not about accuracy. In 1992 Carcanet published a virtually complete volume of Clarice Lispector's newspaper chronicles, up to 1973, under the title *Discovering the World*, translated by Giovanni Pontiero. A selection from that translation was published in the USA by New Directions. In 2022 New Directions in the USA and Penguin in the UK published a new translation, by Margaret Jull Costa and Robin Patterson, under the miserable, tiresome title *Too Much of Life: Complete Chronicles* (which it really is not, as some entries appear to be missing, and not only those whose omission is justified along the way in a footnote – though there are a few added entries from other, post-1973, sources, and an interesting afterword by one of Lispector's sons). Why this new translation? Pontiero's original, clearly a labour of love, has a beautiful clarity, with absolutely appropriate cadences; it never jars. The new translation often does. Too often one is brought up short by a thoughtless, questionable tone. It is, in this respect, not that well written. Read any entry and then go back to Pontiero's translation, if you can, and you will see.

Emma Tristram writes:

You quote Peter Popham under your editorial in *PN Review* 262. He said that in the editorial in issue 261 'you seem on the verge of saying something. Then in the gnomic final paragraph you funk it.'

The editorial in 262 is similar. You say 'This is not the case with the poetry of some of our voluble necropolis-averse contemporaries'. The referent of 'this' is not clear – is it 'how the poem says is what the poem says' (the previous few words)? You go on: '...who nourish their art on an imagined future rich in relevance and leave the realised past ("a circumflex over the kidney beans") well buried. They don't *leave it behind* [your italics]; they have not gone that way.'

So as well as being voluble and necropolis-averse, their 'how' is not their 'what'. They imagine a future rich in relevance. And they leave the realised past well buried, without leaving it behind, because they have not gone that way.

The past you seem to wish they hadn't left buried is illustrated by a quote from *Bouvard et Pécuchet*, which you were making gentle fun of earlier in the editorial.

This is gnomic. I'm trying to work out what poets you are wanting to criticise and why.

By not saying more, you risk leaving the impression of someone wincing at modern trends but not wishing to give details for fear of being censored!

Michael Schmidt replies:

Thank you for your letter. I appreciate there is a problem. There are certain things that, if one says them boldly, will close down discussion with a large part of a constituency. And said boldly, that very boldness may falsify them. I would speak more bluntly in a one-to-one discussion with someone I knew. But when one is addressing a readership which can't answer back, to 'funk it' (which isn't what I intended to do) is not dishonest: the in-your-face statement is never quite what one means either. At seventy-five I come with a lot of luggage: verbal memory, education, things which I value and do not in any way regret; knowledge, ditto. I cannot call on that authority as 'authority' when I am talking with people who are resisting or rejecting the traditions that inform my writing and editing. I want to remain in contact with readers from whom I learn so much: what I try to do is to suggest that there are values which retain value, that we learn a great deal poetically – formally and thematically – from the living dead, and that no aspect of culture is exclusive to any one person or set of people. A love of form, and of the adequacy of enactive rather than or as well as declarative language, is always hard to advocate in an age when personal narrative seems in danger of displacing all else. I didn't mean to make fun of Bouvard and Pécuchet except in the ironic spirit of Flaubert himself: their failed experimental garden is a wonderful creation, and hilarious, too. One of the tones I like best is the one that avoids earnestness... he says earnestly.

The poets who I feel sell themselves short are those who, given their grievances, deny themselves so much pleasure and resource. Diversity means adding to, enhancing, not subtracting and cancelling what still gives.

I appreciate your letter and tone. I agree there is a problem of expression. I have probably said too much here but I hope I have not given offence. I do wince at some modern trends, as you tactfully put it, because they seem to me to lead to diminution... Others of course add wealth.

News & Notes

In Search of Enheduanna, the Woman Who Was History's First Named Author · 'She Who Wrote', an exhibition at the Morgan Library and Museum, New York, until 19 February, explores the world of an ancient Mesopotamian priestess who wrote with 'a strikingly personal voice'. This is the farewell exhibition by Sidney Babcock, the longtime curator of ancient Near Eastern antiquities. 'Ask people who the first author was, and they might say Homer, or Herodotus. People have no idea. They simply don't believe it could be a woman' – and she was writing more than a millennium before either of them. 'Enheduanna's work celebrates the gods and the power of the Akkadian empire, which ruled present-day Iraq from about 2350 B.C. to 2150 B.C. But it also describes more sordid, earthly matters, including her abuse at the hands of a corrupt priest – 'the first reference to sexual harassment in world literature' according to the show. 'It's the first time someone steps forward and uses the first-person singular and gives an autobiography,' the curator said. She was discovered in 1927 by excavators in Ur, daughter of the king Sargon of Akkad, wife of the moon god Nanna and a priestess. Her surviving work includes forty-two temple hymns and three stand-alone poems pieced together from more than 100 surviving copies made on clay tablets.

Remembering the Mexican poet David Huerta · *Adriana Díaz Enciso writes*: On 3 October this year, just a few days before his seventy-third birthday, the Mexican poet David Huerta passed away. It's impossible to overstate the dimensions of the loss that his death means for poetry in the Spanish-speaking world, for contemporary poetry as a whole, and for cultural life in Mexico – particularly poignant when independent thought in that country is under siege from the paranoid chambers at *Palacio Nacional*.

Huerta was born on 8 October 1949, the third child of Efraín Huerta, a major poet himself from the generation formed around the *Taller* magazine, which was so influential in shaping Mexico's contemporary letters. To follow his vocation as a poet with such an imposing figure as a father was no mean challenge, but David rose to it fearlessly, developing a wholly personal voice nurtured by his voracious reading of diverse traditions, and invigorating the Latin American neo-baroque movement.

His earlier books distinguished him as an outstanding poet, but his consolidation came with *Incurable* (1987), a 389-page vertiginous descent into the underworld; a portent of imagery and daring where consciousness and language, on the edge of delirium, struggle to apprehend reality. Huerta continued to grow as a poet and critic, with each of his more than twenty books a renewed attempt at subverting language to express the ordeal and wonder of being human and spiritual in a material world.

Huerta received all major Mexican awards. Poets of younger generations used to approach him with awe, but he put them at ease with his curiosity, modesty and humour. An indefatigable teacher of poetry, loved by several generations of students, and a generous champion of colleagues and younger authors, he taught us how to read the poets of the Spanish *Siglo de Oro*, how to read Neruda and, mostly, how to read the world as a poet.

Being a committed left-winger didn't impair his critical insight into the flaws of the left or right. It was as a poet and not as an ideologue that he wrote about the 1968 Tlatelolco massacre (which he survived, having been demonstrating in the *Plaza de las Tres Culturas* that fateful 2 October) and the disappearance of the fortythree Ayotzinapa students in 2014. His columns in the Mexican press up to the week of his death were an invigorating source of lucid thought, of illuminations on poetry, as well as an uncompromising interrogation of the status quo. He died as a voice dissenting from the current López Obrador's government.

With his surviving wife, the author Verónica Murguía, he established a stronghold of love and loyalty ever revolving around the passion for literature.

'I appeared in the blood of October' – the poem on the Tlatelolco massacre (in Mark Schafer's translation) begins. It was, however, in the light of October that David Huerta was born, and in that light he's left us mourning him, yet celebrating the inexhaustible wealth of his work and the memories of a generous friend and teacher.

Venezuelan poet Rafael Cárdenas awarded the 2022 Cervantes Prize · Born in 1930, Rafael Cárdenas has been a brave poet, staying in his native country through political thick and (mainly) thin, a figure of the left who has watched the left consume itself time after time, writing poetry, aphorisms, essays and autobiography in ways that illuminate his country's history, a series of hopes and wakes. The Premio Cervantes is among the key awards for Spanish literature, and Cárdenas follows in the (recent) illustrious company of the Uruguayans Ida Vitale *and* Cristina Peri Rossi, and the Spaniards Joan Margarit and Francisco Brines.

In recent decades, one eulogist declared, the presence of Cárdenas denas has acquired an almost heroic moral weight in his country. Like his Cuban laureate predecessor Dulce María Loynaz, he decided to stay at home, choosing an inner exile, manifesting his dissidence. In 2014 he emerged from retirement and gave a reading in

Caracas on behalf of political detainees oppressed under the Nicolás Maduro regime, and in memory of those who had died in the troubles of that eventful year. During this period he referred to Hugo Chávez and then to Maduro as 'that man', refusing to use their names. The writer has not been applauded or acknowledged by the political or cultural authorities on his reception of the award, a neglect for which he is clearly grateful.

Edwin Morgan *redivivus* • *A.B. Jackson writes*: Back in 1986, Scottish poet Alexander Hutchison (only two years back on home turf, after living and teaching on Vancouver Island since graduating from the University of Aberdeen in 1966) brought his enthusiasm for poetry-audio projects to the Edinburgh scene to which he was acclimatising. With his Uher 4200 Report Monitor (two 5" reels, 1/4" tape) he began recording poetry readings at the School of Scottish Studies and one-to-one sessions in poets' homes, to launch a 'cassette magazine' called *Bonfire*. Only one cassette was ever produced, featuring Norman MacCaig and Hamish Henderson among others. As the literary editor and archivist of the Hutchison estate I was given access to a pile of his CDs, one of which contained all the original reel-to-reel recordings from 1986–88 converted into MP3 files. Among them, a 25-minute recording of Edwin Morgan reading at his home in Whittingehame Court, Glasgow, 4 May 1988, which was never used. Newly edited to omit coughing fits and false starts, it is finally available to hear at www.youtube.com/watch?v=nLALODXRymk.

David Scott (1947–2022) • *Neil Astley writes:* We are saddened by news of the death of poet and priest **David Scott**, aged seventy-five. David was renowned for his dedication to both vocations. He was being cared for at the Gilling Reane Care Home in Kendal in Cumbria where he had been living since 2019 after falling ill with Alzheimer's disease. Before he died – just before dawn on Friday 21 October – his wife Miggy and children Adam and Lucy played a chant for the *Nunc Dimittis* familiar to all of them: 'Lord, now lettest thou thy servant depart in peace, according to thy Word', then 'grant us a quiet night and a perfect end'. They said their goodbyes 'to the gentlest and best of men' with priest Angela Whittaker from St Mark's Church, Natland, where he is to be buried.

Norman Nicholson wrote that 'David Scott belongs firmly to the long tradition of parson-poets that goes back at least as far as George Herbert… For all their reticence, there is a compassion in these poems and a sense of propriety.' Springing from ordinary events, or a picture, or an aspect of the priestly life, David Scott's beautifully restrained poems work up the detail into a moment of significance. They are rooted in an English culture which is found not only in locality, but also in understatement, and the sideways look. But his poetry has wider reverberations, exploring spirituality and ways of praying as well as momentary glimpses of meaning caught in everyday life.

In 1978 David Scott won the *Sunday Times*/BBC national poetry competition with his poem 'Kirkwall Auction

Mart'. *A Quiet Gathering*, his first book of poems, was published by Bloodaxe Books in 1984, and won him the Geoffrey Faber Memorial Prize in 1986. His second collection, *Playing for England* (Bloodaxe, 1989) was a Poetry Book Society Recommendation. Both books were illustrated by Graham Arnold of the Brotherhood of Ruralists. The poems from the two collections were republished with new work in David Scott's *Selected Poems* (Bloodaxe, 1998), and followed by *Piecing Together* in 2005. His retrospective, *Beyond the Drift: New & Selected Poems* (Bloodaxe, 2014), drew on his four previous Bloodaxe titles, with the addition of a whole collection of new poems.

Ruth Bidgood (1922–2022) • *John Greening writes:* Any poet approaching their centenary loses some readers, but Ruth Bidgood's was once a familiar name – especially as a woman poet in the 1970s, which was when her first three collections appeared. If bookshops outside Wales were more likely to stock Pitter or Fainlight, at home she was popular and would eventually be honoured by the Welsh Academy and Aberystwyth University as well as featuring in the prestigious *Writers of Wales* series. A glance at her 2004 *New & Selected* (from Seren, like much of her work) reveals preoccupations not dissimilar to Gillian Clarke's, with something of R.S.Thomas (for whom she wrote the elegy, 'Bereft'). Although she was not a confident Welsh speaker, Welsh themes – people and especially places – dominate her collections from *The Given Time* (1972) to *Time Being* (2009) and all the late pamphlets.

Born near Neath, Ruth Bidgood read English at Oxford before joining the 'Wrens' as a decoder – chiefly in Alexandria – and later worked on Chambers's Encyclopaedia. But her poetry, when it emerged (in Coulsdon, which she left for Wales after a marriage breakdown), would need no encyclopaedia and little deciphering: accessible, economical, with spiritual reach, it offered an unforced lyricism and a variety of voices, finely crafted though formally unambitious. She could be anecdotal but not confessional, keeping herself in the background, preferring to look closely, to speculate and remember, elegizing landscapes, recalling the folklore of hawthorn or a fifth-century legend. There is the occasional celebration of 'now': a 'Church in the Rain', an 'Earth Tremor' or eclipse, a watched hare, a 'Sheep in the Hedge'('that woolly maniac would hate you/if she had any consciousness to spare/from panic.'). R.S. Thomas found his bright field; Bidgood catches one that's 'an odd shape' and ponders its history. Indeed, she produced some admired local histories, but it is the poetry that distinguishes her.

...*imperialist capitalist white supremacist cis heteropatriarchal...* • Professor Sunny Singh, novelist and academic, was nominated for a place on the executive of the Society of Authors. She is reported as having tweeted in 2020: 'I get regular invites to debate on various platforms. I always say no. Because debate is an imperialist capitalist white supremacist cis heteropatriarchal technique that transforms a potential exchange of knowledge into a tool of exclusion & oppression.'

Reports

Touch and Mourning

Part 2: That Small Word

ANTHONY VAHNI CAPILDEO

'Are you hungry?' Sujata Bhatt asks, in *The Stinking Rose* (Carcanet, 1995). How hungry are you? It is said that we hunger for touch. 'Stinking rose' is a name for garlic. Bhatt's question hints at this hunger for touch. Yet the enticement is by odour and taste. What we cannot see – for the papery bulb of garlic tells us nothing, till cut, crushed or heated – leads towards what we can touch, what we can eat, what becomes us, what perfumes us. Hunger for what is invisible, yet tangible, is not the same as mourning. Yet it is akin: an intensity, transformative, teased away from the possessive, classificatory sense of sight.

Touch is a small word, but it is the leading sense in Ian Duhig's 'The Ballad of Blind Jack Metcalf'. Touching the tombstones engraved with words about the dead – the dead, near but not-themselves; rendered unhugged, unseen, by burial – becomes a way into a whole world of language and people.

> Verse by the numbers, numbered years
>   summing up the dead;
> small fingers feeling headstone faces –
>   how young Jack learnt to read.

The grim social comment, between the lines of *The Blind Roadmaker* (Picador, 2016), is that this boy has stones for teachers and school friends. Being without company is not the same as being in a state of mourning; but if the reader wishes, they can mourn the loneliness of Jack's childhood. Fingers meet stone. The warm tracing in the poem makes us shiver, as the child apparently does not.

Entering the world of Amy Key's *Isn't Forever* (Bloodaxe, 2018) brought on another reading experience that resembled sensation. The words took me out of myself and flattened me into the velvety furnishings of modern loneliness. Would I say they 'touched' me? Have you never felt physically different, coming out of a book? Here the rea-

derly feeling of touch is part of a struggle against flattening. The poems' effect is both comfortable and abrasive, like being pressed – pressing oneself – into good pillows in a precariously rented room. These poems are too wild to constitute mourning for the lack of a lover, or tender friend. To let them 'touch' you is to find yourself at bay in a stylized, two-dimensional jungle of peeling vintage wallpaper. If you want to feel a little resistance – the push that launches a dance into partnered twirls – you must place your hands against those surface patterns, making a dance partner of the wall. Here, the lack of affectionate, intentional touch leads to the body becoming hyper-present to its non-human surroundings. This hyper-presence to oneself as an untouched creature amidst tangible objects is a feature of acute solitariness, and thus part of the poetics of mourning, though *Isn't Forever* is not a book of lamentation.

Absence need not flatten, nor grief petrify. I am keen to explore a poetics of jumpiness. Active mourning for presence can make us thin-skinned. When experience repeatedly confirms what then becomes an acquired expectation of not being touched kindly or at all, we need a language that lives on its nerves. This sensitization textures our daily life in unsayable ways. For many, this is how ordinariness feels. How to write it, without sounding monstrous? Yet it is insufficiently imagined into literature, except via the monster. My sequence 'The Monster Scrapbook' in *No Traveller Returns* (Salt, 2003) was one way to approach how the uncherished body, hyper-present to itself, extends into fragmented, overwhelming awareness of other things, other bodies. At the hairdresser's, the sink against the neck asserts itself like an execution block. Warm water burns. Hot water seems to freeze. The head massage during the shampoo disturbs, as if the skull is being trepanned by ectoplasmic hands.

Does this sound excessive? I would argue that the absence of whatever we conventionally mean by that small word, 'touch', leads to the excess that is another face of accuracy. As multiple translations of one 'source text' lead to multiple perspectives, aren't there different truths to be gleaned from multiple apprehensions of one 'source touch' – including the complexity of that deceptively singular source? While self-forgetfulness is part of empathy, (self-)isolation may sharpen appreciation of the other's sheer otherness. It is impossible to exaggerate what is already absolute. So, we remember for itself what we encounter as its exceeding self, as we experience it through our excessive selves. Contact, not as an act of communication, but a crashing into translation.

What, anyway, is a touch, or the touch – rather than 'touch' in the abstract – for each of us? Certainly, it is not the same as intimacy. The small word suggests a point, not a line; a pat, tap or dab that happens in a moment. Concentrated or casual, can it arrive otherwise than by the overlapping of bodies? Can the 'touch' of a voice be more intimate than the contact that the skin can flinch from, and the mind minimize or intensify? On a Zoom or WhatsApp call, you are out of reach of the aerosol spritz from between the speaker's lips. You are nonetheless susceptible to the sound waves which, by muscular effort, emanate from the other's body. These are real forces, as the military use of sonic weapons demonstrates, no less than the theory behind Sanskrit mantras. Tuning in to the person who is speaking to you is much more than the imagination agreeing to twangle its guitar strings and conjure up your interlocutor. Sometimes the physicality of their speech, highlighted by the narrow focus of a screen, may move you silently, helplessly, and internally to mimic the expansions, contractions and releases resulting in their words. Always, the other's voice can play you like a musical instrument. Your very bones resonate with their faraway breath. Absent, they touch profoundly.

Harmonizing at this level with another's voice is sympathetic. It is not necessarily erotic. The erotics of non-touch touch are, if anything, overrepresented in the western canon, at least until the mid-twentieth century. Consider John Donne's lines: 'Our eye-beams twisted, and did thread / Our eyes upon one double string'. Quoted without context, this image from 'The Extasie' could suggest that the sense of sight enjoys hierarchical primacy over the sense of touch. In fact, touch and sight are not giving way to each other, here. They are mixed into each other. For half a millennium, Donne's words have made the feeling of connection palpable, and suggested the commingling of the two lovers' beings. For the non-reader of Plato, Donne's imagining may seem strange – or it may not. 'We like sepulchral statues lay; / All day, the same our postures were, / And we said nothing, all the day.' This passionate abstention from speech and committed stilling of bodily motion through a stretch of time is akin to – therefore intuitively recognizable from – any loving practice of submission to shared presence, until sheer oneness and sheer otherness embrace and veil what keeps individuals distinct.

What does it mean, that love 'interinanimates' the souls of this couple? Surely not just that they refrain from grabbing each other? No; it is a way of resisting that intensified yet fragmented awareness, which we saw above in bodies that feel isolated, therefore hyper-present in unconnecting ways. It demonstrates willingness to infuse extended time and respectful distance into a mutual sense of the potential of touch, thus magnifying the scope of touch.

All the sadder and more estranging, then, the popular fury of frustration whipped up from the start of the Covid-19 pandemic. That assumes entitlement to immediate touch, and the equation of loss of immediacy with loss of intimacy. The erotics of non-touch touch happen all too literally through long-distance technologies, and the intimacy of holding on together to silences. Sarah Jackson's *Crossed Lines* telephony project is a marvellous poetic resource on this subject. Mourning, touch, absence and presence have things to say, in ways we have just begun to listen.

From the Archive

from *PNR* 258, Volume 47 Number 4, 2021

from Borderline Ghazal

I swore I told no body
but swearing holds no body.

This body holds fast somehow
exile patrols nobody.

Beholden, believed body
you touched, held cold no body. […]

REEM ABBAS

more available at www.pnreview.co.uk

Grey Gowrie

ANTONY GORMLEY

Composed to be read at his memorial service at St James's Piccadilly, 27 September 2022

Calls come unexpectedly; down the line that keen patrician voice with its conspiratorial tones always announcing the prelude to something exciting.

What was it about Alexander Patrick Greysteil Hore-Ruthven, 2nd Earl of Gowrie that gave him such convening power? Could've been the name but once you got beyond the name there was so much else: in speaking (and loving) those syllabled words always with an emphasis on vowels, inquisitive, expectant, anticipating dark eyes framed by big dark rimmed spectacles.

He absolutely brought people together – I remember a lunch when Grey was chairman of the Arts Council. He was trying to get to and connect with the creative spirit of the nation. Sally Potter was there working on *The Tango Lesson* among other musicians and artists. The themes were written as an agenda: real discussion, nothing sloppy. How can art continue to make its demands on us without us making demands of it?

I always thought of Grey as a kind of buccaneer Conservative. He was in there a member of the establishment but on the side of artists, egging them on but also asking for more, asking for the best, asking for better than the 'already done'.

He was both convenor and instigator: imagine a bus careering down the western edge of Lake Como, artists and poets aboard grace of Drue Heinz and her Hawthornden 'Conversazione'. David Sylvester asks, 'Who is the greatest living British painter?' – exactly the sort of game that Grey liked. Peter Porter, Danny Abse, Michael Schmidt, Andrew Motion, Simon Armitage are on the bus. Some pitch in names, some just listen. Frank Auerbach seems to be losing to Howard Hodgkin, some seem to favour Lucian Freud over David Hockney but Grey had sided with Hockney until Sylvester declares that Gilbert and George are the greatest living painters of the modern age which Grey accepts with delight – because he delights in the unexpected (and in breaking rules).

Grey was a Celtic fringe man and played his life like a gambler, and this border-dweller border-raider approach was what made him such an exciting companion. Immersion followed by deep consideration was the order: adventure in foreign intellectual and emotional lands followed by a return to base and philosophical consideration.

Probably the best thing that we did together – or that he helped me to do my best at – was the Angel of the North, a suitable border project for a border man. Maybe Grey saw how the form of body to wing evoked the transition from Thor's hammer to the Cross and how the sculpture could both recognise and heal divisions between north and south. He certainly saw that it could do something for a community, told by his old boss Maggie that it had no future in a Milton Friedman competitive liberal economic world view long before I did. He made sure that, having got lottery money and a European Regional Development Gran, we got the top-up cash we needed from the Arts Council to see it through. That photograph by Nick Danziger (another artist friend whom he brought to the table) says it all. Grey in a Loden coat on a blustery day kneeling in front of this newly arrived rusting work, his arms mimicking its 54-metre wide wings still only just attached at the root.

Grey without poetry is impossible to imagine – a form of poetry that sometimes feels like a shuffled family album of black-and-white images with some rendered in the emotional colour of a place or event, some elegiac, some irreverent and jokey, but all with an eye for reference – literary, geographic – or the appreciation of a detail that brings us to be there, to be with him. The work is always his own experience and always sharp and complex.

Grey's character as a border raider, boarder crosser and division healer was most powerfully written in his body, and it is in his poetry that he describes this borderland:

> we live between consciousness
> and sleep, fly autopilot –
>   night walking, day drifting –
> until the lights go out
>   as almost they did for this one
> who will soon reappear and find
>   the operation persuaded
> his cortex to change its mind.

The poem ends:

>   A domino. A man
> died and his heart and lung
>   helicoptered to shelter inside
> the cavity of this young
>   man who lent me his heart
> in turn that January
>   night of the operation
> in two thousand A.D.

Typically, in Grey's way he made his lucky escape the basis of a determined campaign to support Harefield Hospital and its ground-breaking coronary unit – and introduce me to the world of Magdi Yacoub and his revolutionary heart surgery. With Grey's support this resulted in a work that stands on the hospital roof looking up to the sky as well as to also a wonderful association with Magdi and a realisation that science is as creative as art.

He came back from the edge 'Dark and dangerous still and risky'. He got a new heart and got a new life. Here's his summing up of the miracle of the last twenty years in the borders:

> It is time to dig deep and clean up
> litter of generations who chose to stop
> in this Welsh farmhouse one sly mile from England.
> South-faced to give the sun a chance to soak

into the bones of the living, for summer's sake;
long limbed; Square on the hill and built to stand
in full valley view, proud and plain;
sometimes the house of peacocks, Tye Bain
is our beginning for the end of life.

Grey's was a life that exemplifies the construction of powerful independence through the reconciliation of opposites. He was the last minister of culture who was truly an artist himself, who believed in what art could do, and embodied it in his own life. We will continue to love him as we did when he was amongst us: an inspiration, with an indelible sense of vitality and fun and a belief in the everlasting adventure of life itself.

Tony Wild's *Landscape Collages*

LUKE ROBERTS

Born in Staffordshire in 1941, Tony Wild has been showing his exuberant, sombre work for six decades. Whatever his medium – oil paintings, watercolours, photography, ceramics, collage – Wild is in the landscape, responding. He grew up in a working community of mines and kilns and canals. This is an aesthetics of soot and chalk, dirt and glaze, shimmer and ornament and use. Catching the strange damp light of the Midlands, the beauty of it, the immediacy of perception cuts across the sediment of history and memory. He has clay and coal under his fingernails. What he sees is delicate and subtle; it emerges from a deep intimacy, a long knowledge of his surroundings.

I first came across Wild's work on the front covers of a handful of small press poetry books. John Temple's *The Ridge* (Ferry, 1973), with gorgeous blues and browns; the glowing yellow of Roy Fisher's *19 Poems and an Interview* (Grosseteste, 1975). The cyanotype wraps of Veronica Forrest-Thomson's *On the Periphery* (Street Editions, 1975); a cover for the programme of the Six Towns Poetry Festival, organised in the potteries by Nicholas Johnson in the 1990s. Most recently, he provided a collage of shaped birds cut from photographs of stone surfaces and sky for Tom Crompton's pamphlet *bait-time* (Distance No Object, 2019).

Wild's connection to the poets came through Keele University, where he worked alongside Fisher and Andrew Crozier. Poets would often visit and give readings and talks. Wild became close friends with Barry MacSweeney, keeping up a lifelong correspondence and exchanging artworks and poems. Around ten years ago I visited a room in Newcastle University where MacSweeney's library was preserved along with some of his belongings, including examples of Wild's artwork. I spent a happy afternoon flicking through books, watched over by a large collage of torn paper in three parts, dark bronze and slate.

At his recent exhibition at the New Vic Theatre in Newcastle-under-Lyme, Wild presented some thirty-five collages. The earlier works on show, such as *Urban Interior* (2016) are 'pure' collage, made of six or so paper elements and mounting strong juxtapositions of colour and shape. The visual texture is pleasurable: clean cuts rub against heavy torn edges, and we're aware of the different actions and decisions that go into the arrangement.

Ripped photographs, which appear consistently in Wild's work, bring with them a dynamic temporal residue. There's the original speed of the shutter click; the slowness of development; then the quick jabs of tearing and sticking.

But more recent works tend, as far as I can tell, towards a kind of surface work of double exposure: augmenting, sharpening, and playing with a relatively stable background print through the addition of oil pastels and watercolour. These marks are as sudden and decisive as they are playful. In the undated *English Landscape,* Wild takes a relatively vacant portrait of fields and hedgerows dotted with oak trees and beeches and adds a hard horizon of yellow, loops of purple and teal, scratches of orange. Most of all he adds a zigzag seam of carboniferous black. Perhaps this, too, shares something of the torn photograph's dynamic: these are the slowly accumulated gestures of a lifetime, ringing on the instant.

In one of the larger works, *Voices* (2021), Wild coats torn paper and card in three bands of horizontal colour. The lower section is a shoreline of figures in blue; the middle brings together sailing boats and a brick wall in green, and the upper third in bright yellow slides between abstract shapes and a portrait in hard profile, all ear and neck. It's a complicated image that resolves in bold oscillation. The paint is diluted and thinned, so that the vertical stacking of images seems to softly ease out to the edges. One of the striking aspects of Wild's collages is that his biggest of them tend to feel smaller and more modest than they are, and the same holds true in reverse. It takes time to recognise the density.

Running to catch the train up to Stoke on a wet November morning I grabbed a couple of books from the shelf: Gerard Manley Hopkins and Blaise Cendrars. They turned out to be perfect company, a kind of mulchy cubism. Though there's a melancholy to Wild's work, there's also steady optimism and the occasional ecstatic flash, like the square *Winter Sun* (undated), where everything vibrates with ghostly energy. On the train home there were two passages in Hopkins's journals I kept coming back to: one where he's talking about how cedar bark smells differently in sunlight and in shade, and the other where he's describing bluebells. Running through the senses, he takes us by surprise: '...then there is the faint honey smell and in the mouth the sweet gum when you bite them'. After Tony Wild's collages I know exactly what this means.

Travels on the Loop

CLARA DAWSON

On Google Maps, it's a thin green line tracking the A6010 across south Manchester. Switch to satellite view and it's more of a grey arrow-streak, fringed with cauliflower trees like a toy train set. A carved-out corridor, the inversion of city space from green fields to Victorian railway line and back to trees again. Since the pandemic, cyclists have reclaimed it from the gangs who used to leap out of bushes to steal the bikes from under them. On this sunny spring afternoon, violet bluebells pop and white blossom drifts as I cycle through. My cheap electric bike stops propelling if I cruise so I'm caught in an insistent rhythm, no meandering as the tarmac rolls beneath me. The Fallowfield Loop, the name a swerve that takes me arcing out of diesel fumes and into embankments of April's neon green. Surely there are no such straight lines in nature, I think. But it's better than my home patch in Levenshulme, where green space is a planter of stunted rosemary outside a café on the Stockport road.

I've been reading John Clare's poetry lately and this old railway line laid down in the Industrial Revolution makes me think of him. A Romantic poet who found exquisite beauty in the tiny world of a yellowhammer's nest or the glorious detail of an insect's wing, Clare was distraught at the loss of connection with the natural world that his era heralded. His poetry is shadowed by the Enclosures of the early nineteenth century, when landlords realised they could make more profit by shifting rural labourers off the land, upending their rights to common land. Dispossessed, they made their way to the cities to become the urban poor, living in slums that mushroomed to make Manchester the city it is today. Returning to his poetry, I sense he understood what was coming, the trampling of the small – human, animal and plant – in favour of the rich and powerful.

Hurtling along, I imagine trains rattling by with their burden from coal mine to factory. The murky coal steam of the past seems to haunt the bird-singing present. As my legs push lightly on the pedals, I try to move to the rhythm of Clare's poem 'Crow', reciting it silently. He pictures for us the world as a bird might see it, woods and fields unfolding beneath its flight:

How peaceable it seems for lonely men
To see a crow fly in the thin blue sky
Over the woods and fealds, o'er level fen
It speaks of villages, or cottage nigh
Behind the neighbouring woods – when march winds high
Tear off the branches of the huge old oak

I love how the leap into the crow's vision opens up the landscape so differently to the grounded human eye. I try to mimic it by picturing my own progress along this linear avenue from the perspective of the city's crows. But Clare's vision is not an entirely happy one. Although initially 'peaceable', the 'thin' sky and 'lonely' men speak of a place diminished, a region divided into man-made parcels of levelled fen, village and field. There is destruction in the air, as the huge old oak is torn in pieces. The crow becomes the teller of the tale, able to sketch out the lie of the land as it is shaped by human markers of field and cottage. It offers another viewpoint to map the new boundaries created by draining the fens or fencing off once communal land.

Through Rusholme now, a gap briefly reveals skyscrapers and dangling cranes some way off in the city centre. Villages have burst into cities, cottages to high-rise flats: we are so much further down the line from Clare. Dizzied by the poem taking me into the past and up to the skies, I re-focus on the present. Brambles and shrubs clamber in a scraggly heap up the embankments. A thrush makes a quick diagonal flight across the path. Back in the branches, its white and brown dappled chest fades into camouflage and I lose it. A flash of blue and yellow as a bluetit rounds off the bluebells' colours. The trees are plump with new leaves, reaching to each other across the path to make a tunnel of green. I race through, these encounters passing in seconds, and remind myself of Clare watching the crows at a more peaceable speed:

I love to see these chimney sweeps sail by
And hear them o'er the gnarled forest croak
Then sosh askew from the hid woodman's stroke
That in the woods their daily labours ply

Clare lays out the rhyme so that the crow and woodman live side by side: the crow's croak matched by woodman's stroke, it sails by as the woodmen ply. He famously doesn't use punctuation, signalling his roots in a largely illiterate labouring culture, so it feels as if there is no separation between crow and man. And there's that lovely onomatopoeic 'sosh', an old dialect word for a dull, heavy sound, capturing the swish and swoop of the crow's wings overhead. My own ears are full of my bike's rattling, drowning out the intimate sounds of other creatures on the Loop, so I slow to a halt, laying my bike next to the brambles and resting on a sculpted wooden seat.

I try to tune out the grumble of distant traffic and catch

the noises in the trees and undergrowth. As I listen, I think about Clare's woodman. Is he chopping wood for his hearth to keep his family warm? Or he is a labourer contracted to cut down forests for the great enterprises of the British Empire, wood for shipbuilding or for the iron ore furnaces in factories? A poem that starts off in a rural setting soon unravels its connections to the encroachments of humans. The woodman's actions travel into my present, the deforestation and urbanisation of two hundred years flashing by to land me here, in a narrow passageway of green cut through the city. Trees' health depends on their ability to communicate through crackling roots and the chemistry of smells. I look again at the trees reaching out at branch level across the tarmacked path and realise there is no wild commune for them. Instead, perhaps a desperate straining against the materials we have parked in their way.

I look down and see metallic laughing gas canisters tramped into the soil, impacted down with other fragments of rubbish, beginning their long wait to become future fossils. The thought of such deep time makes my stomach dive, and I watch the pollen drifting. I imagine myself as a speck of pollen, hitching a ride on the insects whisking through the air, just sailing by like Clare's crow. A magpie snapping through the brambles brings me back and then a crisp packet near it crumples. I step towards it, taking care not to squash the bluebells, hoping to get closer to its mate. It's not another magpie, but a brown rat, hustling away with a fine tail behind it.

A thrush, a magpie, a bluetit and a rat. A gift to see so many other creatures on my journey and a reminder of the joy that Clare teaches us to feel.

> I love the sooty crow nor would provoke
> Its march day exercises of croaking joy
> I love to see it sailing to and fro
> While feelds, and woods and waters spread below.

He finds pleasure in what others might find ugly or common. Despite the 'sooty' colour and 'croaking' noise, words hardly associated with nature's beauties, he loves the crow. His enjoyment of the crow's free-wheeling flight contrasts with his own place in the fields

and woods. If labourers were fenced out of the land that had belonged to them, at least the crow is not hampered by these borders.

This afternoon, I share this feeling of freedom as I fly along the Loop, released from the constraints of traffic and the boredom of slow bus journeys. But as I bounce over a lumpy patch of tarmac, I start to question what unseen barriers might lie around me. For the birds who sail high in the skies above Manchester, roads and houses and polluted canals now spread below. They remain free to fly across them, but what does this freedom truly offer when the loss of habitat makes their lives precarious? And I start to realise what I share with them. I too am an animal who must travel the linear route laid out for me in a cityscape fragmented by its industrial history. I see myself and my fellow human animals hemmed into the narrowest of green spaces as land is clawed away for the city.

In the last couple of years, I've followed campaigns for wildlife corridors between nature reserves, offering safe passage to animals surrounded by urban conglomerations. Roaming hedgehogs who need us to cut holes in our garden fences, badgers and adders who rely on networks of hedgerows. Are these remnants all we can cast to them? I try to imagine what it's like to find your way home blocked by a fence or railway, your food source dried up or polluted. Only when we start to see the world through the eyes of our fellow animals, as Clare does, will we understand how we've carved and re-cast our landscapes.

Clare writes about a county and a country caught in the grip of industrial progress, but a world in which birds still offer a different way of envisioning the places we inhabit. Cycling along the Loop with his poem in my head has taken me off my narrow human path, the rhymes and rhythms allowing me to dive and swoop with the crows. A reaching beyond, the ancient Greek sense of ecstasy, *ek-stasis*, to step outside myself into the godlike perspective of a bird. I cross the tram line and pull up at the end of the Loop, heading to meet friends at a Chorlton bar. But I'm left wondering, with only scraps and corridors left, how long will birds be able to provide us with such inspiriting visions?

Letter from Wales

SAM ADAMS

We recently spent a few relaxing days at Aberaeron, in essence a small Regency-Victorian era town built with neat precision and now spread out in colourful variety, about a harbour just half-way round the bight of Cardigan Bay. Our visit coincided with the second summer heatwave and we were grateful for occasional cooling breezes off a millpond sea. The sunsets were splendid, though not quite as dramatic as those I sometimes witnessed

sixteen miles further up the coast during student years at Aberystwyth. Then, viewed from the Prom against a glorious curtained skyline of shimmering reds, the mountains of the Llŷn peninsula curved round, stark black, like encircling volcanic islands risen from a gilded sea.

The first-year syllabus of the English course at Aber in those days included Thomas Love Peacock's *The Misfortunes of Elphin* (1829). I still have the copy (printed 1927!)

I bought new at Galloway's bookshop in 1952. Underlinings and marginalia prove I gave some time to it, and I well remember its account of the drowning of that fertile demi-paradise *Cantref y Gwaelod*, the lowland hundred, due to the neglect of the drunkard Seithenyn ap Seithyn Saini, whose duty it was to ensure maintenance of the embankment that kept back the often choppy waters we viewed from classroom windows of the Old College building on the seafront.

Aberaeron is the expanded realisation of the vision of one man – an Anglican cleric, born at Cenarth, a short distance down the road south – who, having acquired two adjacent estates by marriage and inheritance, left his Hampshire parish to return to Wales. The Rev. Alban Thomas-Jones Gwynne (1751–1819) saw the potential commercial advantage of a port serving the broad hinterland of Ceredigion and Carmarthenshire. In 1807, he obtained by Act of Parliament permission to build the harbour, with wharfs and storehouses, at the mouth of the river Aeron, and to levy tolls for its use. Construction continued till 1816 and cost him a little more than £6,000. The harbour now provides berths for a multitude of sailing craft, mostly unmoored for weekends and holiday jaunts, but it continued to receive trading steamships into the early 1920s.

Gwynne was not the only visionary entrepreneur active on the west coast of Wales at the end of the eighteenth century. William Alexander Madocks (1773–1828), from Denbighshire, via Jesus College, Oxford, and a Fellowship of All Souls, became MP successively for Boston, Lincs. and Chippenham. In 1789, a handsome inheritance from his father enabled him to buy the Tanrallt estate, Penmorfa, some seventy-three miles from Aberaeron, in that northern corner of Cardigan Bay where Llŷn juts into the Irish Sea. There he enclosed 1,000 acres of *Traeth Mawr* ('Big Beach') and embarked on ambitious plans, first to build the town he named, with justifiable pride, Tremadoc (Madoc's town): housing and all that was essential to support a population, including a Town Hall, an inn, an early powered woollen mill, and a fine property for himself, 'Tan-yr-allt', on the hillside overlooking the site. In 1807, he obtained by Act of Parliament permission to build an embankment across the Traeth, diverting the river, Afon Glaslyn, to enclose a further 3,000 acres, a scheme he knew had first been mooted by Sir John Wynn of Gwydir two centuries before. His hope that a toll road alongside the embankment would carry mail between London and Dublin was dashed when the preferred route via Holyhead on Anglesey was announced. Yet another Act (1821) enabled him to construct a port at the northern end of the embankment which, without a blush, he named Portmadoc – it eventually served to export, among other items, slate from Blaenau Ffestiniog quarries. Madocks invested a fortune in these speculations and, had all worked out as he hoped, might have gained another, but like a number of notables of the period he ran out of cash and was pursued by creditors. Tan-yr-allt was ceded to one blessed with the Dickensian-sounding name Girdlestone. Trips abroad might have brought some relief, but on his way back from a visit to Rome he fell ill and died in Paris in September 1828.

Having stolen her willingly away, Percy Bysshe Shelley married Harriet Westbrook in Edinburgh on 29 August 1811, but they didn't settle to married life there. They were doomed never to stay in one place for long, journeying from the Lake District to Ireland, and on to Lynmouth, Devon, where Shelley wrote and, in singular ways, 'published' his *Declaration of Rights*. There, realising they were being watched by spies and in danger of being apprehended, they crossed the Bristol Channel into Wales and pitched up finally at Madocks's great works on Cardigan Bay. There, it was a case of all hands to the pumps following the breaching of the embankment by the spring tides of February 1812. Enthused by the project, Shelley took an active part in raising money for it and, finding that Tan-yr-allt – with that rare modern wonder, a WC – was tenantless, notwithstanding his impecunious state applied for and obtained the lease from Girdlestone. What happened next is well known and yet uncertain. On the night of 26 to 27 February 1812, Shelley was (or alleged he was) shot at through a window at Tan-yr-allt. As Richard Holmes, in his monumental biography, concedes, it is certain he suffered a profound shock and at once gathered up his ménage and fled.

The previous autumn, negotiating with Girdlestone in London, Shelley had met Thomas Love Peacock at the home of bookseller-publisher Thomas Hookham. That both had travelled in Wales and had reasons to return may have assisted their bonding. In any event they became close friends. During several months he spent in north Wales in 1810–11, Peacock had visited Tremadoc, where work on the embankment was nearing completion, and then settled some six miles away at Maentwrog. A considerable autodidact, adept at learning languages, he would hardly have neglected the opportunity to gain an acquaintance with Welsh. Some evidence of this appears in *The Misfortunes of Elphin*, and his efforts may well have enhanced his acquaintance with Jane, daughter of the local rector, the Rev. John Gryffydh. They formed an attachment which endured over distance and a lapse of several years, before (one supposes) Peacock's appointment to a secure post at India House in 1819 stirred him to propose: the pair married in March 1820.

Back in 1812, with north Wales still on his mind, it is unlikely that Peacock would have missed the news that Madocks' grand embankment had suffered a breach and that fund-raising efforts were in train to repair the damage. From his time at Maentwrog, he would also have become familiar with the old story of the drowning of *Cantref y Gwaelod*. The seeds of the stormy opening of his narrative were sown. A written version of the same tale, naming the miscreant Seithenyn, resides in the mid-thirteenth-century *Black Book of Carmarthen*, though it clearly originates much earlier. All just a myth, of course, except that I read in the *Guardian* (22 August) of the Gough Map in the Bodleian Library at Oxford, dating from much the same time as the *Black Book*, which clearly shows two substantial islands that formerly existed out there in the inscrutable waters of Cardigan Bay.

Sand City in the Rain

HORATIO MORPURGO

Mother and daughter spend most of *Put the Rubbish Out, Sasha* talking to or about their deceased husband/father, who often appears on stage with them. A career soldier who died from heart failure, he is here now because of a 'sixth mobilisation', in which even the dead are being called up. Under the terms of this mobilisation, however, those recruited can only report for duty with the permission of loved ones.

As they talk the past over with their spectral visitor, through this grieving and recalling, they try to envisage a future. What boundary between an inner life and the outer world survives the experience of war? In any case, no, he does not have their permission. They can't afford another uniform. Or another funeral.

The playwright, Natal'ya Vorozhbit, is from Donetsk. Her play is set during the earlier phase of the war, from 2014, but if it ought to feel out of date, it doesn't. It is witness of another, more durable kind than reportage. London's Finborough Theatre is small but it was full the night we were there. I for one emerged from it asking why had I been checking my phone for six months – or why are we, rather, in the mass, so ready to prioritise reportage over other forms of witness?

*

Travellers to Ukraine are warned not to take photographs anywhere near government buildings, military installations or border infrastructure, because of the 'targeting information' such images can contain. Self-consciousness about pointing your phone at things can spread in unforeseen directions.

In a huge tent in the centre of Chernivtsi, south-west Ukraine, volunteers serve about a thousand hot meals every day. The city, which has thus far escaped attack, is housing many refugees from the east of the country. A woman tells me about the three months she spent in a basement with children and no running water. Her sixteen-year-old son turned grey. Another woman's brother had been missing since he went to fight near Kherson at the start of the war. She had given a DNA sample in case any remains show up. Her husband was fighting, she didn't know where.

I had other questions prepared – what they thought about the war, about Moscow, NATO. Glancing down at them now: a reticence. Sitting opposite people tearing up, the kind of talk I'd indulged in for months at home felt out of place, stood revealed, rather, for what it largely is: a way to keep warm. A way to stay eloquent, make a noise.

I did usually ask and of course they did answer. They had views. Worth mentioning here – they were all Russian-speakers – is that nobody I met expressed anything but scorn for the idea that as such they had ever required 'liberating' by Moscow.

Chernivtsi / Czernowitz is best-known to the outside world as Paul Celan's birthplace and the town where he spent almost half his life. When he wrote against *the garish talk of rubbed- / off experience – the hundred- / tongued pseudo- / poem, the noem*, he was setting himself not against witness as such but only against a certain 'garish' variant or travesty of it. The poet 'challenges the hour, his own and the world's'. He was adamant that his work stood in 'direct relation to reality'. What to make of such a claim, in his home town, at this time?

*

It was Celan's mother who insisted that her son receive a classical German education. Her murder in 1942 in a labour camp in Transnistria opened the void around which his later life and work would revolve. Celan found himself, in 1945, inescapably committed as a poet to the language of his parents' murderers. The reputation for difficulty owes much to later work exploring the boundaries of what is sayable at all in such a 'mother tongue'.

Friederike's determination that her son should be as culturally German as possible arose partly in reaction against her own background, having grown up in Sadagora, a small town just outside Czernowitz. Small town it might be but this was no mere satellite settlement. Rebbe Israel Friedman, a charismatic teacher, had relocated his 'court' after being hounded out of the Russian Empire during the 1830s. He founded a famous Hassidic community: Martin Buber would be taken there often as a boy and the experience was decisive in his later rediscovery of that tradition.

This centre of mystical piety and Yiddish culture formed a contrast with the German language and reform Judaism adopted by most Jews in the nearby city. Whatever the mother's ambitions, the son, for his part, would one day sign himself 'Paul Celan, from Czernowitz, near Sadagora', in a significant inversion of the expected order. Nor was he the only writer to be formed by the tension between these more or less adjacent centres. Aharon Appelfeld was born in the same street as Celan. His *The Retreat* (1984) is a troubled and troubling novel about Jewish assimilation. Rose Ausländer's father was a rabbi in Sadagora, and the town figures in many of her poems: *Trees made out of holy letters stretched their roots / From Sadagora to Czernowitz / The River Jordan, then, flowed into the Prut.*

There were other equally productive tensions to choose from – Ausländer wrote fondly of a town where 'four languages understand one another'. All the online biographical notes notwithstanding, Celan was born in 1920 not in Austrian Czernowitz but Romanian Cernăuți. The city was for centuries part of the Moldovan Principality, was then absorbed by the Polish-Lithuanian Commonwealth and had been occupied by Ottoman Turkey and Tsarist Russia before it was Austrian. Between 1918–40 it was Romanian – as much the town where Mihai Eminescu lived as a young man as it was 'the secret capital of German lyric poetry'.

The largest communities in the city Celan knew – Ukrainian, Romanian and Jewish – made up the kind of sophisticated urban centre that breeds linguists. The 'Café Europa' on its main street is said to have subscribed to one hundred newspapers from all over the continent. Celan knew Yiddish and Ukrainian, was fluent in Romanian all his life and would translate from Hebrew, Russian, French and English. But 'only in the mother tongue can one speak one's own truth'.

Reading one hundred newspapers a day granted no exemption from the mid-twentieth century. Travelling to study in France in November 1938, Celan passed through Berlin on Kristallnacht. He was home again and studying Romance languages when the Wehrmacht and Romanian forces entered the town in July 1941. Cernăuți was Czernowitz once more but the civil administration was left in the hands of its Romanian mayor, Traian Popovici.

'Authorisations' issued by Popovici to thousands of Jews rescued them from deportation and saved at least hundreds of lives. At Yad Vashem a tree was planted in his name.

Does anything of the town's pre-war reputation persist? Refugees and residents alike assured me Chernivtsi had escaped attack because it is not associated with forms of nationalism found elsewhere in the west of the country. Other explanations are possible, but it's true there is no statue to Bandera, though there is one to Eminescu. There is one to Taras Shevchenko, of course, but dismantling the town's memorials to the Red Army only began this year, long after Soviet statues lost pride of place elsewhere in the country. Where might I investigate any such legacy further? Two places came to mind.

*

Many of Sadagora's Hasidim migrated to Vienna then Palestine and London just before the First World War. Its Moorish-style synagogue, built by Israel Friedman's son, stood empty for three decades. It was requisitioned by the Russians for tank repairs during the Second World War and used throughout the Soviet years as a tractor repair shop. A roofless shell by the mid-1990s, the decision was taken by Friedman's descendants to rebuild. Work was completed in 2016, the restoration overseen by Moise Kreis, raised Orthodox in Chernivtsi and a Yiddish-speaker. It was a Saturday when I knocked and he gave me the tour.

None of the old photographs showed what the original ceiling had been like. Kreis chose to have the new one painted blue with clouds, as a reminder of the years when this space was open to the sky. The reference is also to the Feast of the Tabernacles, he explained. Observant Jews build outdoor shelters each autumn to commemorate the forty years in the wilderness. Through the roof of twigs, sky must be visible.

The new ceiling at Sadagora is both a biblical and a historical allusion, then, to deliverance as well as to dereliction and displacement. The building is currently home to forty refugees from the war zone, of which four are Jewish. Such a response to what is most precarious in our world felt entirely of a piece with what I'd heard from volunteers working with refugees in the city centre. 'Poems', wrote Celan, 'are *en route*: they are headed toward. Toward what? Toward something open, inhabitable, an approachable you, perhaps, an approachable reality.'

Moise walks me to through the middle of town to the Rebbe Friedman's tomb and is greeted by a passing group of teenagers. He shows me a statue in the main square, by a local artist, dedicated to the musician who wrote the tune for *Hava Nagila* here. He surprises me also by arguing that the Holocaust in Bukovina began not with the arrival of the Nazis but with the deportation of three and a half thousand Jews, or 'socially unreliable elements', rather, by the Soviet authorities, shortly before Hitler's invasion. 'There is anti-Semitism everywhere', as he puts it, 'but in Russia it is at the state level. Just listen to Lavrov.'

Celan knew what he would term 'anti-Semitism Soviet-style' well and after returning at the end of the war to what was now Russian-occupied Chernovtsi, he promptly made his way to Bucharest, in 1945, where the Communist takeover was still three years away. Exactly where he wrote *Todesfuge* during these years of displacement is unknown. A friend claimed Celan read it to him in 1944 by the railings outside the Metropolitan Church in Chernovtsi. Its first publication, in any case, was in Bucharest, in Romanian. He worked there mainly as a translator from Russian: his suspicion of the country's leadership did not extend to its literary culture. He translated Lermontov then and his later versions of Mandelstam are still read and widely regarded as among his finest achievements.

He crossed the border into Hungary illegally in 1947, making his way to Vienna and then to Paris. He came to know other Romanian émigrés there, Emil Cioran among them. Michael Hamburger argued that the later work owed much to French surrealist influences, absorbed initially through his Romanian context. How far it was multi-lingual Cernăuți, the town 'where both people and books lived', how far the catastrophe that followed, how far it was French surrealism or the mysticism of Sadagora that chose Celan to speak for them will doubtless be contested for as long as he is read.

The contestation has taken a very particular form in his home town. Chernovtsi was, from 1944–91, because of its proximity to Romania, situated in a border zone. This made it even less accessible to outsiders than most places in the USSR. This isolation, in such stark contrast with the pre-war bustle, drastically affected the town's relationship not only with the outside world but also with its own past.

Petro Rychlo meets me outside the gates of the city's literally palatial university (the splendid former residence of the Metropolitan Bishop). He accompanies me to a seminar room in its Faculty of World Literature. Born in Chernovtsi in 1950 and a graduate in German studies from this university, it was not until 1975, he explains, that he came across Celan's work, in an anthology of contemporary Austrian poetry published in Moscow.

The poems, utterly remote from the socialist realism on which he had been raised, were unlike anything he had read before. That they had been written by someone from his own home town, of whom he'd never heard, whose reputation abroad was immense, who had taken his own life in Paris a few years earlier, was a lot to take in at once.

Trying to find out more about such a writer in the Soviet Union was a delicate matter. It wasn't only the elliptical style and all its ambiguities which made Celan suspect to the authorities. His departure from the country also made him a traitor. That he was Jewish was a not unrelated point – in post-war campaigns against 'cosmopolitanism', latent anti-Semitism was an active ingredient. Here, additionally, was a writer in German, a language 'not appreciated at that time'.

Rychlo managed to locate Ruth Kraft, a lover of Celan's from his youthful days, still then living in Cologne. She agreed to send him some of the poetry he had written for her. He translated it and in 1990 organised a celebration of what would have been Celan's seventieth birthday, inviting old Romanian friends, among them *Todesfuge*'s first translator, Petre Solomon. His own earlier wonderment

that such a writer could have been forgotten in his home town was widely shared. The event made headlines. With the Soviet Union faltering, this felt like part of the wider struggle for freedom from its ideological grip.

An anthology, *The Submerged Poetry of Bukovina* (1990), featured others of the German language poets who had once flourished in the region. Rychlo went on to name and help set up 'Meridian Czernowitz', an international literary festival named after a famous speech the poet gave in 1960 when he accepted the Georg Büchner Prize. More of which later. This life-long engagement with Celan's work culminated in 2020 with the completion of a ten-volume bilingual German-Ukrainian edition and a more recent collection of reminiscences about the poet, *Through the Eyes of Contemporaries* (Suhrkamp, 2021).

In naming the festival after the town's German name, Rychlo explains that he meant to invoke the pluralism once held together here by a liberal, late-Habsburg order. The foreign writers who attend are mainly German-speakers, together with Romanians and Israelis. But this is not just an attempt to restore, in Celan's phrase, a 'yesterday worth preserving'. The festival is popular with the town's students and did go ahead this year, though it was called a 'meeting' instead, given the sombre context.

Such have been this scholar's efforts, in the place he knows best, to bring about a world in which different peoples read and reflect upon one another's literature. Outside the synagogue in Sadagora, I mention Meridian Czernowitz to Kreis and there is immediate recognition. 'I know them well', he says warmly, and for all those ways in which they differ, it occurs to me the two projects have elements in common. Related literally through the families of Paul Celan and Rose Ausländer, they arose from a common experience, too. That of growing up here at a time when the city's past was scorned, its contacts with the outside world drastically curtailed and its future on hold.

The decision to rebuild in Sadagora, Kreis explains, expressed a wider hope that Europe's century of warfare and racial persecution was past. Such spare time as Rychlo has is largely spent translating the writers who attend the festival, so that their readings can be accompanied by Ukrainian versions. That kind of dedication has to be drawing on deep roots. In their different ways, both men are working for a future that will be answerable to but not trapped by the century past and its legacy.

*

As war aims, a new 'New Russia' has come and gone but Ukraine's need of 'denazification' has been stuck to through thick and thin. Its purpose (none too subtle but no less successful for that) has been to direct attention to the country's far-right groups, which do of course exist. But its most important effect, I would argue, has been its tendency to obscure or render absurd all those low-key, piecemeal, patient efforts, carried on over decades, in Ukraine and elsewhere, to build a Europe wiser for its catastrophe.

In Kyiv in 2014, the (Russian-language) novelist Andrei Kurkov put it to me like this: 'For a Russian politician it is very difficult to portray Ukraine as an enemy nation.

They use these terms, like Fascist, to create in the Russian mind an image of the enemy. This is difficult because there are millions of Ukrainians in Russia…' For Kurkov, 'denazification' supplies the strong rhetorical liquor needed to dull perceptions of the world and of people as they actually are.

I've carried that around ever since and still think there is much to be said for it. It occurs to me now, though, hearing this trope once again tirelessly repeated, that to slap it down, however deservedly, for the absurdity it is, is both to follow a multitude and to miss an opportunity. There is a longer and a better answer we can give it, one which begins, as such an answer should, elsewhere.

*

The man became a sieve, the Frau / had to swim, the sow, / for herself, for no one, for everyone – / The Landwehr Canal makes no murmur. / Nothing / stops. The plaque to Karl Liebknecht is next to a lake in Berlin's Tiergarten. There's a memorial at the spot nearby where Rosa Luxemburg was thrown dead or dying into a canal. Sprayed in fluorescent green on the bank opposite is the following, in English: 'DON'T WORRY ABOUT THE THINGS YOU CAN'T CHANGE'. Can it be that someone passed this way, failed to google either of them and hadn't read his or her Celan, either? Is public art any measure at all of what people remember?

It is not, in any case, the only means of reminding available. Half an hour's walk away, *Albert Speer in the Federal Republic* is an exhibition about Speer's self-reinvention after his release from prison in 1966. Hitler's architect and armaments minister repeatedly maintained, for example, that plans for the Final Solution had been concealed from him. He had known nothing of conditions in the camps.

Scholarship long ago tested these and other claims and found them to be false. The current exhibition's theme is, rather, why Speer's 'memoirs' blossomed into best-sellers and even movies in the Sixties and Seventies. Why West Germans needed so badly to believe this telegenic, plausible penitent.

Jean Améry survived his time in a camp established by Speer. He published an open letter, explaining that he had not read Speer's books and would not do so. Silence, he suggested, would be a more convincing expression of remorse than any 'gesture in the limelight'. His letter made little headway against the TV appearances and rave reviews by celebrated figures. Speer's legend flourished because it exonerated. If so senior a figure as Speer could say he didn't know, then 'we', too, after all, might be in the clear.

Entry to the exhibition is free. It is located in a low, steel, oblong structure. The large empty area around it is covered in track ballast. At intervals along tarmac walkways are information panels telling you what was where. The entire site, known as 'The Topography of Terror', was once occupied by central administrative buildings of the SS and Gestapo.

There were in 2021 an average of three anti-Semitic incidents per day in Berlin. State-funded *Erinnerungskultur* [culture of memory] is not a cure-all. But it is an attempt. That exhibition illustrates well how agonisingly slow this process can be. Its displays form part of a difficult, continuing effort to show that resistance to the truth may take the form even of agreeable fellows like Speer. This is neither a memorial in bronze nor a 'gesture in the limelight' and is all the more credible for it.

*

The temptation to play games of trite equivalence should be resisted but even Solzhenitsyn, a writer allegedly revered by the Russian president, arrived at staggering figures for the number of people who perished in Stalin's Gulag. It is always the right time to begin the process of reckoning with one's own authoritarian traditions. Always some plausible talking head will be explaining that the fault lies elsewhere and always did. Always on offer some thrilling stridency in which people can lose themselves *instead*.

*

Silence, cooked like gold, in / charred / hands. Even as noblesse was obliging Albert Speer to give his innumerable interviews, Celan hesitated to take his post-war celebrity in Germany at face value. Even with recent additions, his prose statements amount to little more than the slender volume published by Carcanet twenty years ago. Was his reputation a form of moral laundering? Why could he never feel at home in Germany? The school-text status of *Todesfuge* failed to reassure. The repetition of 'ladies and gentlemen' in his Meridian speech led John Felstiner for one to suspect the blackest of concealed ironies.

But Celan is not the only writer educated by Cernăuți to whom we might turn in our efforts to get some longer view on the present. Gregor von Rezzori, son of an Austrian administrator, treated his own youthful anti-Semitism and that of his milieu with a frankness which, misunderstood at first as avowal, upset many. An autobiographical novel about his childhood there, *An Ermine in Czernopol* (1958) is among the earliest novels in German to celebrate what we might now call multi-culturalism.

The story ends just before the outbreak of the Second World War. At its climactic moment, rioting breaks out after a football tournament between teams representing the different communities. When the district governor, keen to make his mark, orders soldiers in to restore order, a man is killed. The Romanian mayor, one of the book's heroes, disagreeing with his superior over this decision, gives expression to his love for the city. 'The idea of order as perceived by the military mind', he argues, does not apply in such a community:

'[T]he only true love is the approving kind, the kind that lets something be the way it is… To create order in Czernopol would mean to kill Czernopol… because I see our infamous street-character as one of the primal forms of the great Eros, as the well-spring of all spiritual fertility. I see in it what I call "the drunkenness of the sober": in a nagging, alert scepticism towards everything, and, above all, itself.'

Those who argue, or used to, that Ukraine is too full of different peoples to be 'viable', take note. As much essay as it is novel, as much a biography of his city as it is its creator's autobiography, *An Ermine in Czernopol* functions also as semi-reliable guide book. Its theme is a city that stood on the edge of so many empires until it found at last a way to make a virtue of the periphery – for as long as Europe would allow it.

*

'Let me now undertake a bit of topological research', writes Celan towards the end of his Meridian speech. He begins 'searching for my own place of origin' on what he calls 'a child's map'. But this is no guide book. Everything is gone. Celan concludes, almost before his search has begun, that 'none of these places can be found. They do not exist. But I know where they ought to exist, especially now, and... I find something else.'

What use is it, then, literally seeking out the physical place, when 'the place of origin' he had in mind was so clearly an imaginary one, quite other than this palaver of hotels and trolley buses and steep streets? He had said it repeatedly: the only thing that remained 'secure amid all losses' was language. And the 'something else' he finds now is closely related: 'immaterial as language, earthly, terrestrial, in the shape of a circle which, via both poles, rejoins itself... a *meridian*.'

*

In the end, wrote Yehuda Amichai of his friend, the words grew so heavy in him that *God laid you down like a heavy load, maybe just for a moment, to take a breather*... With a relentless clarity Celan would qualify even the nature of that language which had remained 'secure'. To be valid now, he wrote, any language 'had to go through its own lack of answers, through terrifying silence, through the thousand darknesses of murderous speech.'

The Russian President was addressing the nation for the first time since launching his invasion. It rained heavily that day and I had been in Chernivtsi for a week. Huge flags on either side of a little man renewing his threat to use nuclear weapons. A week and I still had not been to see the poet's birthplace. Nothing might depend on the house or its plaque but needing a walk I waited for a lull and went.

Cobbles were streaming and part way along Ukrainska Street a flock of pigeons was crowded along a ledge beneath the overhang of a tin roof. Unsure if I had missed a turning, I asked at a stationer's: a customer just leaving showed me the rest of the way. She explained that German had been her favourite subject at school. There's a website that helps you practise languages. Her son was still here but her grandchildren had all gone to stay with relations in America.

Each of us, I suppose, searches for some image of what is worth persevering with or preserving, to get a sense of scale, to hold up alongside the little man with his flags and his bomb. Wasn't that it? Chatty strangers or streaming cobbles. I was here to learn how far this town lives up to its side street with a plaque towards the lower end. Or was it for its pigeons sheltering on a ledge?

As his seventieth birthday in 1990 played its part then

so now on sale at the Meridian Czernowitz bookshop is *Paul Celan 100* (2021). In Ukrainian and German (all texts are in both), writers discuss what the poet has meant to them: as witness, archetypal refugee, mystic, Ingeborg Bachman's lover, Heideggerian with hesitations, drinking companion. Its pages are testimony in abundance to a town more than living up to its tree-lined side-street.

The remaking takes many forms. Berlin-based artist Helga von Loewenich travelled to Bukovina as soon as it became accessible againfrom 1991. Elaborately decorated well-heads are found on many of its farms, often tricked out like miniature Buddhist pagodas. Intrigued, von Loewenich only later became aware of the frequent references to these in the poetry of the region. Her book *Wasser: welch ein Wort* (2019) is based on an exhibition of her work on this theme, put on in Chernivtsi's Art Museum in 2014.

Across from each poem with its well, river or cloud motif, there is a water colour on the facing page. The title is taken from Celan's *Sprachgitter*: *Above, soundless, the / travellers, vulture and star, / Below, after everything, we / ten of us, sand people. Time, / how could it not, time has / an hour even for us, here, / in the sand city. / (Tell of the wells, tell / of the well-wreath, well-wheel, of / well-rooms – tell us... / Water: what / a word. We understand you, life.) / The stranger, uninvited, from where, the guest...*

*

'Reality is not simply there, it has to be searched and won.' His may not be the mannerisms we associate with 'engagement', but he told a gathering of writers in 1962 that his poem *Engführung* was addressed to 'Atomtod', or the threat of nuclear war. A theme we have not, after all, succeeded in putting behind us. *Gales. / Gales, from the beginning of time, / whirl of particles, the other, / you / know it, though, we / read it in the book, was / opinion / Was, was / opinion...*

The reference is to a book about Democritus in which the poet had been shocked by the phrase: 'Nothing exists but atoms and empty space, everything else is opinion.' He described himself in a letter at the time as 'tormented by anxieties, atomic and other'. Any 'music' the poem set this to must somehow manifest the scale of the incoherence and distress: *the world, / a millicrystal, / shot up, shot up / * / shot up, shot up. / Then nights demixed... / no / flight shadow, / no / measuring table, no / smoke soul ascends or joins in.*

To 'touch' the meridian, as he put it, is it to meet a person, travel to a place, to read or write a poem? Some or all? 'This week', shrilled the news anchor, stirred by her president's speech, 'This week marks either the eve of our imminent victory or the eve of nuclear war!' Perhaps we'll know we have touched the meridian because we will feel, momentarily, the 'thousand darknesses of murderous speech' lose their grip upon us and therefore, in some infinitesimal way, upon the world.

*

'Forgive us that we carry flowers. Forgive us that we breathe,' intone mother and daughter at the graveside, in *Put the Rubbish out, Sasha*. Russian tanks are on the border. Anticipating invasion and attacks on infrastructure, they take delivery of a wood stove. The daughter is expecting and they worry about how the child will be delivered. They buy in enough petrol to get to Warsaw if necessary. They re-open an old well.

Poems

OKSANA MAKSYMCHUK

Sasha Dugdale writes: Oksana Maksymchuk is a scholar and anthologist, co-editor of the ground-breaking *Words for War* (https://www.wordsforwar.com), which gives voice to a whole generation of exceptional Ukrainian writers in translation. Oksana herself is that rare thing: a bilingual poet. An author of two collections in her native Ukrainian, she also began writing poetry in English in 2016. This recent work, a response to the last eight months of war in Ukraine, resembles in form the poetry she writes in Ukrainian, with a pared-back and songlike structure.

Water Under the Bridge

No more bridge now
but the river
flows as it did before

like a single tear
rolls down the face
of the landscape

tears through the terrain
laid out for it by another tear
and another before it

Doesn't grieve when the towns
clustered atop its banks
lie in ruins

Doesn't weep
cradling the corpses
toying with the remains

Indiscriminate
like a poem's flow

reflecting everything
changing nothing

House Arrest

I've been writing this note
for a couple of minutes now
Still there's no response
I'm so angry

A vision came
bearing a gift
It was moist and sweet
smelling faintly of plumbum

How dare you abandon me
alone in a room
in a house with strangers
in a city popping with guns

All that keeps me whole
is the memory of the meal we share
every Friday night
and the candles we light

Promise we'll make it again
peeling roots
in the kitchen, stained hands
passing a knife, a potato

The room forms
around me, listening in
to my fear
and not as a friend

Under its oculus, I strip
naked, I whir, my heavy wings
rustling with each *plié*
like lowered shutters

Stolen Time

Trapped in a plan
of another's making
we're squandering time
awaiting the war

Perfectly formed evenings
of navigating between the dark
silhouettes of trees
against the purple snow

Weekend afternoons of
urgent love-making, voices
seeping through half-drawn curtains
adorned by shadows of

migratory birds –
jubilant and remote
citizens of a world
shared in shards

Non-Gentle Reminder

when my fluttering heart
takes off
its awkward perch
within my ribcage

let me at least remind you
to button up your coat
and put on the red hat
I got online

to help identify you
in the current of the crowd
in case the enemy strikes
by air, by land, by water

Rocket in the Room

what the rocket has in common
with the room full of children
is its current location

somebody thought the rocket
belongs in the room with children
and now it's here

in time
someone else will come
and collect the pieces

of the rocket and of the children
weeping and shouting insults
at the sky

but for now
this rocket and these children
are an unsorted matter

a puzzle
awaiting a solution

Rose

It can't happen to me
until it does

The trajectories meet
on point

Terror comes off
layer by layer

Glowing inside
the cellar

supple serrated petals
pushing against the war

here it is – the Rose
I'm dancing here

Samurai Cat

They will recognize him
by the tattoo of a samurai cat
on his ankle

blackened, yet still
clearly discernible
despite the burns

He sat out for a long time
in the summer heat
before they collected him

When he finally arrives
at his destination
they plead with his mother

not to unzip the bag
showing only
a single foot

Shell-shocked, she obeys
without listening, lays her lips
on the plastic

Drone Footage

When a shell strikes a person
there's a scattering

resembling a flock of birds
taking off

hands flying in the air
signalling

feet levitating
in mid-kick

their avian shapes
casting shadows

lithesome and carefree
from on high

Kingdom of Ends

In the brief intermission between the
world wars
we somehow managed

to weave a language
out of the things we felt
mattered

for our future
as an impermanent species

Barely even words but
collections of signals from
distant planes of existence, patterns

expressive of a communion between
roots and surfaces, sprawling networks of
fungi, projectiles of spores

shooting out like smart
self-navigating missiles

propagating a form of rebirth
that would touch us all

impartially, indiscriminately

Four Poems

BERTOLT BRECHT

translated by Timothy Adès

Thoughts of a Gramophone Owner

I bought it in 1904, a really good purchase
Ever since, in the daytime it's been my habit to hide it
It's a thrilling wooden box for life's darkest hours
With the voice of Adelina Patti inside it.

Adelina Patti, the singer: died 1911
I have her voice (may the earth lie lightly above her)
From the life, I've kept the receipt from when I acquired it
Her voice is still good, I'll be playing it over and over.

No doubt it'll sing to my grandchildren too, one day
Adelina's the name it's always answered to
Once I fell over from drinking too much brandy
So my dear Adelina's voice isn't quite like new.

But it still is special and quite clever people have marvelled
That somehow life comes up with so many things
We've certainly made enormous technical progress
She's there in the box and it's La Traviata she sings.

In our great-grandparents' time it couldn't have happened
So much artistry, which we were unavoidably wasting
We've made such progress for good as well as for evil
Such a machine is a sort of life everlasting.

George often says: Bring some tobacco and Adelina,
I'm so depressed – and large as life she appears
And sings Traviata, his face turns really respectful
She's sung only Traviata these eighteen years.

I might quite often have bought some other records
My wife from the first would have liked a shimmy or two
But I've always steered away at the very last moment
I think multum non multa, keep all my applause, Adelina, for you.

A Fish Called Fash

There was a fish whose name was Fash
He had a tree, a snow-white ash
He had no hands to mobilise
For work, his face contained no eyes
His brainbox held no implements
He also had no common sense
He didn't know his one-times-one
Of all the countries he knew none
He simply was the fish called Fash
And had this tree, the snow-white ash.

He saw men build a house, and hew
A heap of wood, and tunnel through
a mountainside, and brew a skilly.
Fish Fash just sat there, looking silly.
And when they asked him, What are you?
Tell us what sort of work you do,
He told them: I'm the fish called Fash,
This is my tree, my snow-white ash.

They went indoors come eventide
And Fish Fash followed them inside
They sat beside the stove. What do
You think he did? He sat there too

They brought the steaming skilly-dish
There with a big spoon sat the fish
And loudly said, Eat up, let's dash
And you shall see my snow-white ash.

They laughed and let him eat and yes
Quickly forgot his idleness
Until a famine had begun
A major not a minor one
All must bring food to beat the shortage
Cheese bread and someone brought a sausage
But Fish Fash brought the spoon, no more.
Some people bridled when they saw

And asked Fish Fash: And you, they said,
Tell us what you've contributed?
Replied Fish Fash
Well, I suppose my snow-white ash...

At long last angry with Fish Fash
They scolded him. Their words were harsh
They chucked him out with quite a crash
Through the oak doors and hacked to bits his snow-
     white ash.

Murder Ballad of the Reichstag Fire

Tune: Murder Ballad of Mack the Knife

Thirteen years on end the Drummer
warned the world of coming crime
perpetrated by the Commune:
hasn't happened all this time.

And the little drummers grumble:
something, happen soon – it's time!
Trouble is, you see, the criminal
types will not commit the crime.

On the towpath – it was winter –
people gathered, lingered there:
for today, remarked the Führer,
Reichstag Fire is in the air.

On that very Monday evening
stood a lofty house in flame
such a dreadful crime, and no-one
knew the perpetrator's name.

But a youngster was discovered
he was naked to the hip
from his lining they recovered
book of Commune membership.

Ask by whom this book was given
why the dolt was standing by
all those Brownshirts in the offing
nobody to ask them why.

How to set alight the building
with twelve men it could be done
it was burning at twelve corners
and was mostly made of stone.

Twelve fires burning: in amongst them
stood twelve Brownshirts, quite a squad
pointed with their blackened fingers
at the feeble-minded lad.

So it happened that the Führer
cracked the whole conspiracy
and the whole ensuing story
shocked the great majority.

In the house where the conspiring
was unarguably planned
lived a person, name of Goering
unaware and ignorant.

He was Chairman of the Reichstag
he dismissed the sentinels
when he heard 'The Reichstag's burning'
he of course was somewhere else.

Kindly tell us Mr Chairman
why you sent the guards away
after all, that very Monday
was the Reichstag's burning-day.

If he could be cross-examined
he would struggle, to be sure
but he can't be cross-examined
he's a cross-examiner.

He won't cross-examine Goering
truth and lies he will not hear
takes no evidence, averring
that the Commune's guilt is clear.

Long before the sun had risen
February night of blood:
shot to pieces or in prison
all the anti-Hitler brood.

Likewise Roman Caesar Nero
Christian blood was to his taste
so he set his Rome a-blazing
soon in ash and fire effaced.

Thus he proved it, Caesar Nero
Christians, villains one and all
and a certain Hermann Goero
learnt of this when he was small.

1933 one evening
Monday night in Berlin town
Reichstag had no further meetings
for its house had been burnt down.

This was sung by Oberfohren
short his life, the man who sang
when the world was told the story
he was nobbled with a bang!

The Thirteenth Sonnet

The word you've frequently reproached me for
Comes from the Florentine vernacular
Where Fica signifies a woman's privates.
They scolded Dante savagely because
He used it in his verse, great though he was.
I read this morning how he was reproved
For this, as Helen brought abuse on Paris,
Who came off rather better, as it proved!

You see, then, even gloomy Alighieri
Was caught in the controversy that mars
This thing which otherwise receives applause.
We know it, and not just from Machiavelli:
In life and books alike, we fight our wars
Over the place we justly write *** ******.

'Stelle', Italian for 'stars', is the last word of the Inferno, the Purgatorio and the Paradiso, the three parts of Dante's Divine Comedy. 'Stelle' is also a German noun meaning 'place', and Brecht has wittily put this word last in his poem.

The asterisks may be read as 'with stars' *or* 'con stelle'.

Bertolt Brecht (1898–1956) was a champion of the hard left, a great playwright, and above all, a great, versatile, universal poet. Thanks are due to the Brecht Estate and Suhrkamp Verlag for permission to publish these translations. The original poems appear in *Bertolt Brecht, Gedichte in einem Band* (Suhrkamp, 1981). A book of Brecht's poems with translations by Timothy Adès is due to appear after copyright expires on 1 January 2027.

Universals and Particulars

ROBERT GRIFFITHS

The world is made up of particulars. So, if one were trying to represent that world in writing one might hope to capture something of that particularity. One might do this by referring to an immediate sensory experience: 'I heard a cough / as if a thief were there...' (Alice Oswald, *Fox*), or to a specific object, in a specific context:

It was the first gift he ever gave her,
buying it for five francs in the Galeries
in pre-war Paris...
(Eavan Boland, *The Black Lace Fan My Mother Gave Me)*

In this way, particularity seems important, perhaps even crucial to certain kinds of poems.

Plato, the first ever literary critic, nevertheless decided that it was a profound weakness in poetry that it was too preoccupied with particulars, and not enough with the universal. He thought of a poet as representing, for example, only a particular love, and not the universal, LOVE. The latter, apparently more important thing, he saw as the concern of the philosopher.

In a very obvious way, though, Plato could not have been more mistaken about the character of poetry. For poets are users of words, and words, as was noted by a much later philosopher, do not refer to particulars. They refer only to universals. John Locke, the eighteenth-century philosopher who wrote the first sustained treatise on the nature of language, was puzzled by this oddity – that while the world consisted of particulars, the vast majority of words signified universals: 'All things, that exist, being particulars, it may perhaps be thought reasonable that words, which ought to be conformed to things, should be so too, I mean in their signification: but yet we find the quite contrary. The far *greatest part of words,* that make all languages *are general terms...*'

Take Oswald's poem. The word 'cough' for instance, does not refer to a particular cough. There is a good reason for this. If the meaning of 'cough' was a particular cough, then the word could not be used to communicate with anyone unacquainted with that particular. So the world 'cough' has a general meaning. Even when I use it to refer to a particular cough with a phrase like 'I heard a cough', you do not understand this word because you are acquainted with this particular, but because you have a general concept 'cough', which you associate with the word. The implications of this for poetry, indeed for writing in general, are clear. It means that in a poem, particulars are never present. Particulars do act as prompts to writing, but when we write, they instantly disappear into the cloud of general meaning created by general words.

After Plato, Aristotle, the first person to write a sustained critical work about poetry, proposed – contrary to his teacher – that poetry is actually concerned with the universal. However, he muddled this correct insight by claiming that access to the universal in poetry was *through* the particular. This message was to ring down the centuries, inspiring a poet like William Carlos Williams, who averred, 'That is the poet's business... in the particular to discover the universal', and opening *Paterson* with, 'To make a start, / out of particulars / and make them general'.

What Williams's mantras and Aristotle's theory obscure is that when writing, the poet is *obliged* to signify the universal. So it is otiose to encourage poets to do this. Aristotle's suggestion that a poet might arrive at the universal *through* the particular is misleading. For, in the poem, the particular is not present so cannot serve as a route to the universal. A poem is, among other things, a network of universals, a network of general words that signify universals. It may have been prompted by the particular, but the particular then falls through the bottom of the cloud of universality that is the poem.

After Plato and Aristotle, pre-modern critics continued to wrestle with the question of whether poetry is concerned with universals or particulars. Samuel Johnson's poet Imlac, in *The History of Rasselas*, ventures a theory. He notes that the poet must observe everything, 'To a poet nothing can be useless'. Acknowledging that this threatens to sink poetry in a mass of particularity he counters that 'The business of a poet... is to examine, not the individual, but the species'; attention should be given to 'prominent and striking features', and these might 'recall the original to every mind'. Again, there is no need to encourage the poet to refer to the species; she has no choice but do this. Further, what a poem could never do, even if there were an 'original' which it in some way signified, is recall that original 'to every mind'. The 'original', if by this we mean the particular that prompted the poem, is always lost in the poem.

Following on, the Romantics were very concerned with universality, even as they appeared to exhort poets to particularity. Wordsworth's 'Preface to the Lyrical Ballads' proposed that poets should avoid 'abstract ideas' and focus on 'the incidents of common life'. Nevertheless, this interest in particular incidents of common life must serve the purpose of 'tracing in them... the primary laws of our nature'. One was directed to particulars in order to – as Aristotle might have said – discover the universal. In Wordsworth's 'The Simplon Pass', the particulars of nature become indeed 'the types and symbols of Eternity'.

While advising poets to avoid 'abstract ideas' may be considered sensible, this does overlook the fact that the mere choice of a word consigns a poet to at least the use of a *general* idea. In this way, a level of abstraction is inevitable in writing. It is well known that Wordsworth's famous daffodils poem was prompted by an experience of some particular daffodils, of which his sister also wrote in her journals. But these 'originals' are not recalled to every mind by the poem; they were in fact doomed as soon as the word 'daffodil' was written down, in both the poem and the journal. What was triggered in every mind was a concept of daffodils.

Coleridge, who was more philosophical than Wordsworth, considered this issue in some depth. He had begun by accepting the view of the English empiricists, such as Locke and Hartley, that we have access to sensory particulars and that it is only from these that we developed concepts. But then, having read the German idealists – all of whom writing under the influence of Kant – he concluded that the mind cannot passively receive particulars. Instead, experience was created by the action of mental universals – Kant called these categories – on raw sensory data to which otherwise we have no access. Our experience of a particular is only possible because we place them under universals.

For Kant, the faculty that united sensory data with mental universals was the intellectual-sensual imagination, and this led to Coleridge's own theory of the creative poetic imagination. Coleridge accepted the Kantian view that each experience was already the application of a universal, and he declared that a poem was therefore a linguistic representation of an intellectual-sensual synthesis, of universals acting on particulars (and in Coleridge's case, some 'feeling' thrown in for good measure). Poetry could not therefore be, as the 'Preface to the Lyrical Ballads' had suggested, about particulars being *raised* to the level of universals, for universals were already necessary in order for there to be any consciousness of particulars at all.

Interestingly, the modernist poetic revolution of the early twentieth century rather ignored Coleridge's insights and partly defined itself in terms of an escape from universality. While the generalising energy of the great Romantic poets was treated with a certain respect, modernist critical fire rained down on their Victorian successors, whose allegedly limp generalisations were seen as drifting too far from the particular and the actual. Swinburne was regarded as a prime example of what too great a concern for the universal might do to an unwary poet. T.S. Eliot thought Swinburne obsessed with the mere word, ignoring the object that apparently lies somewhere behind it: 'When you take to pieces any verse of Swinburne, you find always that the object was not there – only the word'. Yet it is interesting to read this comment in the realisation that in the poem the object is actually never there, only the word and its associated concept, and that to this extent all poets necessarily share in Swinburne's apparently distinctive failing. In none of them is the object still there; there are only words.

F.R. Leavis, who was not averse to swiping at the great Romantics, notoriously chastised Shelley for his 'weak grasp of the object' and how in the 'vague general sense of windy tumult' of 'Ode to the West Wind', 'there is no object offered for contemplation'. The problem is that in a poem an object *cannot* be offered for contemplation. Ezra Pound claimed he wanted to 'paint the thing as I see it'; Ford Madox Ford urged 'the rendering of concrete objects'; the 1913 Imagist manifesto warned, 'Go in fear of abstractions'. William Carlos Williams, seeking as we know the universal in the particular, proclaimed, 'No ideas but in things'. But this mantra conveniently ignored the fact that there are no things but through ideas, and that in poetry, there are actually no things, only ideas, only words, only universals.

After modernism, and its misleading attempt to campaign on behalf of the object, concern for the particular departed from the literary scene with the coming of 'high theory'. The Structuralist view, for example, was that literature was not about objects at all, but about archetypes, which are essentially universals. To this extent, Structuralism is closer to Aristotle than to Leavis. A literary work should not be seen as the attempt of an identifiable individual to engage with actual particulars but rather a closed, conceptual structure, where concepts point independently at one another and not at any separately identifiable world of objects. Building on Saussure's seminal idea of meaning as essentially relational, the meaning of a term was neither the object it referred to, nor actually indeed a single concept, but a whole network of concepts with which it was inter-defined in a web of conceptual relationships. This idea was extended by the Post-Structuralists into the view that, essentially, the meaning of a single term could only be fully grasped – if at all – by an apprehension of the relations it held to all other terms, all other 'signifiers'. This apparently new insight seemed to echo the grand, nineteenth-century Hegelian view that one knows anything at all only by knowing Everything. In effect, all meaning comes to derive from All Meaning, each term's significance coming from what looks like the ultimate universal.

The Post-Structuralist view of meaning did go too far. It is simply false that one grasps the meaning of a term only by grasping its relationship to all other meaningful terms. But it remains the case that the meaning of a term is a universal, and this is already enough, it seems, to prevent the writer representing the particularity that may occasionally prompt her work.

But while we cannot penetrate behind the universality of language to the particularity that may occasionally prompt the poet, perhaps there remains some solace for the writer desperate to suppose that her writing could ever be about the world that fills her experience. One possibility builds on a suggestion made by the philosopher David Hume when he considered Locke's original comments about the universality of language. Hume's suggestion was that while it was correct that we have no access to the particularity experienced by the writer, we do have access to our own. Our concept of 'cough' for instance – to labour this example – will be supported to some degree by our own experiences of coughs. This allows us to reconstruct the particularity that may have prompted the writer. In this way, of course, the sense of particularity we associate with any writer will come to depend at least to some extent on the richness of our own experience of particularity. The power of a poem might then derive not so much from anything in the history of the writer, but from things in our own history. But this fits in well with one of the sharper insights of high theory, that the understanding of a text depends as much if not more on the reader than on the writer. It has also a broader psychological plausibility, that the effect of a work of art on us is dependent more on facts about ourselves than on what might have been intended by an artist. Of course, we can also by analogy suppose that the particularity experienced by an author is of a similar kind to our own. So while we can never recover, for instance, Wordsworth's daffodils, we can suppose that they were not so very different to what we now ourselves perceive. This makes it possible for us to sustain that sense that the writer does at times speak about the world, even with those tools, words, which are so ill-suited for the task.

Like the Ancient Greeks Who Measured Their Wealth in Olive Trees

BEVERLEY BIE BRAHIC

The Plague Year

From the road below his garden
I am talking to Paul.
A pair of plane trees shades our two houses
With their seasoned, common wall;
Cicadas drone *it's hot it's hot*
Till the sun inches down
And a breeze lifts from the Rhone Valley Plain.

All of that I have learned by heart.
In fact it is February, the year 2020
And only a twinge of foreboding
About the pestilence gaining ground
As surely as a cyclist
Climbing the Mont Ventoux.
Paul rakes manure over his beds,
Tough work for a man of his age:
Ninety in October. Last October.

Each morning when he opens his shutters
I hear Paul's screen door bang
All's well with the world, I go back to sleep;
And last thing at night
After he reads the face of the moon:
A moon to plant and a moon to harvest,
A moon to trim trees, a moon to pare nails.

Two rows of spinach left, and the escarole
Whose outer leaves he tosses to the hen
Keeping only the daffodil-frilled white hearts,
Protected from the light of day
Like asparagus, whose purple tips
Will soon be poking up in market gardens.
On Fridays, in the *Marché de Carpentras*
Paul dickers for the broken tips and crooked spears,
Cheaper
Than the straight ones, and there's no waste.

*

Three months go by. At his kitchen window
Paul watches starlings come and go
From their nest in a crook of the plane tree.
'They work hard,' he approves.
Same birds every spring? I ask from the road -
We are keeping our distance –
'Yes,' firmly – and who am I
To question how he knows?
Who planted our two plane trees?
Paul shrugs:
Before his time, before his father's.

One cherry orchard left
And olive trees Paul will never sell
No matter how much they give him
To put houses on the side of that hill.
And the rest, these quarantine days
Comes from the *ÉpiCafé*
Where on Sunday he settles his bill
Religiously: *You never know*, says Paul.

Tomorrow, I say, we'll go to Mazan
To buy asparagus. Slender white stalks
Not being airlifted
To Tokyo and New York and Paris,
Whose restaurants are closed.
Two kilos, Paul says, broken ones: 'I'll pay you.'
I owe a cock to Aesculapius. Pay it, Crito.
On ne sait jamais, Paul is thinking, I think.

BEACON AND LAMP

Anthony Rudolf at Eighty

Compiled and edited by Eric Hoffman

PN Review is proud to honour poet, critic, essayist, memoirist, translator, editor and publisher, Anthony Rudolf, on his eightieth birthday. Rudolf is unique among modern English authors in his ability to move effortlessly between poetry and prose and fiction and non-fiction, yet maintain his unmistakable voice: a voice that can be authoritative and commanding, yet also contemplative, receptive and searching. Proof of his diverse talents is a body of work that includes over forty books, seemingly countless scattered essays and reviews, and extensive correspondences, published and unpublished.

His corpus includes works of fiction; six volumes of minimalistic, philosophically profound poetry; four memoirs (of which the three most recent are centered around his books, objects, possessions and autographs); two critical works on the artist R.B. Kitaj; monographs on his most prized authors and poets (Levi, Oppen, Rawicz and Rosenberg); translations from French (Bonnefoy, Vigée and Jabès), Russian (Tvardovsky, Vinokurov), Hungarian (Heimler) and other languages (Simonovic and Neiger-Fleischmann); edited works (a volume of Jewish poetry, books on Jonathan Griffin, A.C. Jacobs, Keith Bosley and Paul Claudel, among others); and his publication of the diaries of his second cousin Jerzy Feliks Urman, who died at the age of eleven, a victim of the unspeakable violence of the Holocaust.

The two subjects about which Rudolf is most passionate are the atrocities of the Shoah and the Damoclean threat of nuclear war; these were the principal subjects of his much-respected Menard Press, founded in 1969, the catalogue of which includes literary and political texts, works that, true to Rudolf's vision, often effectively blurred the boundaries between the two.

This oeuvre reveals Rudolf as, above all, a student of history, specifically the history of the creatively liberating yet monstrously destructive past century, the paradoxes of which he is able to articulate with a gravitas tempered by humour, grace and wit. A central theme is memory as a vehicle of recovery: Rudolf is as unlikely to refuse to avert his gaze from or to ignore the world's horrors as he is to overlook its fragmentary beauty; to do so, as his work suggests, would be to surrender to the darkness and ignore the penetrative, redemptive light of art. His writing is both beacon and lamp.

Rudolf was for many years employed by the BBC World Service, and was the partner, and frequent model, of the artist Paula Rego, who died earlier this year. He is currently at work on a book-length essay on Rego, the long-time provisional title of which is *In the Picture: Office Hours at the Studio of Paula Rego*. *Balbuciendo*, Rudolf's translation of a sequence of poems by Michèle Finck, is forthcoming from Broken Sleep Books; *Paideuma* is about to publish 'Obstinate Hope', Rudolf's second essay on poetry written or read in extreme situations; and the online magazine *Women: A Cultural Review* recently published an interview with him by Deryn Rees-Jones on the subject of Rego.

Being There: Bruce Ross-Smith

In his tribute to Yves Bonnefoy on the poet's ninetieth birthday in June 2013, Tony Rudolf expressed his 'gratitude' to Bonnefoy 'for being there, always open to dialogue, always awaiting the possibility of learning something new, like all the great teachers'. This writer would certainly echo that tribute to Anthony Rudolf, master-translator, sensitive poet, publisher through the Menard Press of some 170 titles, writer on art, not least the work of his late partner, Paula Rego, literary critic and scholar, editor, biographer, obituarist, reviewer, social critic and political activist. His close friend the poet and biographer Elaine Feinstein wondered at the launch gathering in 2017 for his collected poems, *European Hours*, 'how Tony ever finds time to write his own poems when he is always so busy doing so many other things, including the promotion of the work of others'. 'Being there', ever a benevolent presence across sixty years of devoted hard work on behalf of so many others, Tony, as political activist and as a source of influence, has demonstrated his commitment to the immediate and 'greater' world. Recently he sent me a succinct commentary on what is happening in Ukraine.

Thirty years ago Menard published twenty-one pamphlets on the then nuclear threat, which included contributions from Dan Plesch, Ronald Aronson, Nicholas Humphrey, Joseph Needham, Martin Ryle and Lord Zuckerman, and two from Anthony Rudolf ('Byron's Darkness' and 'From Poetry to Politics')

As he turns eighty there is no chance Tony Rudolf will relax his concerns for himself and his family and for all of us. He is by nature a practicing humanitarian. This might sound glib. It isn't.

> In his song of remembrance
> he sings an ancient song of earth.
>
> Anthony Rudolf, 'Return to Ashkelon'

Jane Augustine

I can't help thinking, these days, of two unparalleled and heart-felt extensions of art and thought by the prolific poet-critic-publisher Tony Rudolf. First, he founded Menard Press – initially to promote translations into English of good writers in other languages. When the Cold War came, however, he shifted ground – see Menard's 'Nuclear List' in the thirtieth anniversary catalogue – to emphasize how nations are competing to build the largest number of nuclear bombs with which to annihilate their neighbours. These stockpiles define our present worldwide political condition. His second unparalleled move, also lasting about thirty years, to my knowledge, was his deep love for and loyalty to the Portuguese-born artist and printmaker Paula Rego, made a Dame in 2010. My husband Michael Heller and I first met both in person in the Islington living room of art-collector friends. Tony and Paula were holding hands. Dan Burt in *PNR* 266 (July-August 2022) says rightly that 'her own history composes the essence of her oeuvre'. Tony was an integral part of that oeuvre as well as, in Burt's words, her 'long-time companion, model and escort'. My favourite and warmest image of them comes from the years in which every night Tony read poems in English over the phone to one of the world's greatest living artists until she died on 8 June 2022.

Michael Heller

Over forty years of friendship. Language is the life-river we have both dipped into. Hundreds of letters, emails, faxes, hours of unrecorded talk in London, and in New York on those few visits by Tony and his heart companion, the painter Paula Rego. We range from the literary to art and on to the political, call and response, occasional argument, sometimes harmonious choral singing. Perhaps some of our extensive verbiage courses through Tony's masterpiece, *Silent Conversations* (2013). Its frontispiece photo of the author amidst his Babel towers of books, spilling across shelves, tables, the floor. 'A Reader's Life', he subtitles the book (but it's even more a writer's life), full of unbounded curiosity, love and empathy. Literature, poetry, translation, especially from the French, Judaism, the fate of Jews, of the world, politics, they are all in the flow. As a reader and responder, I am hooked not only by Tony's brilliance, but by his deep ethical sense of proportion and value, as when he took his distinguished Menard Press out of its literary publishing to concentrate its work on the nuclear disaster facing the world. Not that Menard became any less 'literary' during that time; rather, it refocused with powerful literate writing the disaster we still confront. His writings, whatever the mode, experimental, original, unclassifiable, often fabulistic, as in his most recent book, *Pedraterra & Angleterre*, embody a deep reflective imagination. His life's work – it is all of a piece – as he puts it in a poem, is to be caught up in words: 'lingering alone, / wineglass in hand, pen upon this paper', where he can 'inhale an ancient oneness'.

John Naughton

Anthony Rudolf has been my incomparable friend for many decades. We have collaborated on projects involving poets as diverse as Yves Bonnefoy and Paul Claudel. Tony has been a vital force in the relation of French literature to the English-speaking world, both as a gifted translator and an active reviewer. But his contributions to literature in general extend far beyond his commitment to French writing. As editor of the Menard Press, and through English translations he has published there, he has brought to our attention a wide range of writers and poets from a diversity of literatures and cultures we might not otherwise have known about.

Tony became the devoted friend and confidant of the artist Paula Rego, and I remember moments we shared all together, particularly a memorable dinner on Charlotte Street, after which Paula graciously invited me and Tony to her studio for an after-dinner drink. Tony was a committed and loyal friend to this great artist, and his presence in her life was a great blessing to her.

Tony and I have worked together on a number of projects involving the work of the French poet Yves Bonnefoy. The poet could not have had a more dedicated champion of his work, since Tony was the driving force in the recent volumes of Bonnefoy's poetry and prose published by Carcanet.

I remember my visits to Tony's apartment on Woodside Avenue, outside London, the place filled with so many books you have to navigate a safe passage between them all. The books have been his life's companions.

I was always delighted to see Tony at various conferences and colloquia. His presence always made the events more precious. Ever attentive to and vigilant regarding the political realities of the world around him, Tony is, for me, the embodiment of a caring person, a *mensch*. I salute him on the occasion of his eightieth birthday and thank him for his invaluable friendship.

Deryn Rees-Jones

Tony Rudolf is a writer of great intellect and style for whom deferment, digression and delay has become an art form.

His writing, both poetry and prose – which well deserves the epithet Rudolfian – never fails to surprise me by its range and depth and erudition; and not least its embeddedness in the two passions – passion and compassion. See especially his *Silent Conversations: A Reader's Life*.

Like his late partner the artist Paula Rego, Tony is a brilliant storyteller.

Our conversations over the last decade – in person, on the phone or over email – have been a whole new education in European music, literature, translation and art. Through him I've stepped into new imaginative worlds.

Tony jokes frequently about his role as matchmaker to other writers and as an 'attendant lord'. His pleasure in bringing like-minded people together is only matched by his Macavity-like willingness to disappear once connections are made.

Tony never eschews seriousness. We have a shared fascination with memory, but also a weakness for slapstick. He always makes me laugh.

Along with being a scrupulous editor, Tony is also a marvellous encourager and motivator. I have a special section on my bookshelf for Tony's books. When I'm writing something tricky I often pull a book down and dip in to hear his voice, so he can send me back to a thought.

Though there are so many contenders – his *Journey Round My Flat: An Informal Inventory* (2021) and his heartbreaking book about his second cousin Jerzyk – perhaps my favourite of his books is *Zigzag* (2010).

Tony is also a master of the postscript, a precious gift to the essayist who refuses linearity and favours in his own writing the fragment and the accumulating thought. See above.

One of Tony's many strengths is his capacity for enduring friendships. What a privilege it is to count myself as his friend.

Alan Wall

Tony's mind has many mansions, and he has never let me off the hook. For this he deserves a handsome payment, but he has never sent a bill.

Augustus Young

I have been close to Anthony for over fifty years. Our friendship has been sustained by Sunday aperitifs in London and is now maintained in daily email exchanges to and from France. But I have never taken him for granted. He has so many aspects that I often feel that I'm one step behind him. It has been a harmonious relationship, based on differences that make it interesting rather than contentious. Not least in relation to writing, which is Anthony's driving force.

I have a shelf of his books to which I refer more frequently than any author friend. This is because of their astonishing scope. Hardly a subject that I'm struggling to unravel has not been thoughtfully considered. He cannot be labelled. The nearest one would be to call him a man of letters, but that would date him in another century. Poet, literary and art critic, memorialist, polemicist, creative publisher, collector of poets and artists. All these come together in his trilogy of brilliantly veiled autobiography, *The Arithmetic of Memory* (1999); *Silent Conversations: A Reader's Life*; and *Journey Around My Flat: An Informal Inventory*.

Rudolf communicates the personal indirectly. Books, objects and albums speak for him. But the depth of underlying emotion always surfaces with telling detail. Only in one book is it raw: *Jerzyk* (2016), the history of his cousin who aged eleven killed himself when he thought the Gestapo had arrived. The boy was doing what he was told and took the pill. Reading Jerzyk's precocious diaries Anthony must have felt like his twin. The reconstruction of the circumstances and the aftermath for his parents is painful but compelling, a lost life redeemed by literary means.

As the preferred male model of his beloved Paula Rego, Anthony could be anything she wanted him to be, a decadent priest, a pampered tyrant, Rochester fallen, a saint ascending. I can't wait to read the promised book of their collaboration in life, art and love.

Marius Kociejowski

Several times I have sought the word that might capture, both in what he does and who he is, the subject of this tribute, and each time the answer comes back the same: solidity. And no sooner is that word anchored in the mind than come others, chief among them *trust*. One trusts his mind, his imagination, his judgement and how they manifest themselves in the lifelong project that has been, whether in deed or animus, his steadfast devotion to literature. There has been no self-aggrandisement in it, no hankering for applause, only solidity. In the field of translation, there is his pioneering work on the poetry of Yves Bonnefoy, for example; in remembrance, it has been exemplified in his publication of the diary of his eleven-year-old relative Jerzy Feliks Urman who, when he mistakenly thought the Gestapo were at the door, put an end to his own life; in memoir, its most recent manifestation is the gorgeously eccentric *Journey Around My Flat*, in which he recounts the objects that have had a bearing on his life; in publishing, there is his Menard Press, which has published authors as diverse as Primo Levi and Christopher Middleton; in political activism, we have his campaigning for nuclear disarmament; and in poetry, there is his own. It is no surprise that a man whom I've seen but rarely over the years feels more a companion than a stranger. If one dips into the etymology of the word, a companion is one with whom one shares bread, and, here, he is also the companion who ensures the survival of our fragile culture. Chevalier de l'Ordre des Arts et des Lettres, a chevalier he is also by nature. Anthony Rudolf's presence is required, absolutely.

Barry Schwabsky

There are so many sides of Anthony Rudolf to appreciate: the poet, the essayist, the publisher, and so on; all of them somehow or another impinging on my own work, even if only in a sort of fantasy mode (for instance, I've only dreamed about and talked about starting a press, never done it). But because I've recently begun trying to render poems from Italian and French into my own idiom, it is Anthony the translator whom I think of first these days. And he's been kind enough to give some occasional advice on my (dilettantish but earnest) exchanges with other languages. This work has made a lived experience out of something I'd only previously understood as a sort of intellectual puzzle, the congruence and incongruence of translation, the difference between translating the words and translating the poem. How can that be? After all, we want to say, the poem is made of nothing but the words. But is that true? It's made of words, and of something else – 'As if beyond pure form there trembled / Another song, alone and absolute.' Those lines are from one of Anthony's translations of the poetry of Yves Bonnefoy. It's an encomium to the voice of the great contralto Kathleen Ferrier, and in itself the poem is already a sort of translation: a voice singing, an embodied voice carried over into the implicit voice of poetry – of French poetry, I should emphasize, since Bonnefoy's poem might really be as much about Mallarmé as it is about Ferrier; that poet's recurrent *cygne* makes its appearance here, and even the *glaive* with which he had figured the voice of Edgar Allan Poe, or rather the effect of that voice. Elsewhere, Anthony quotes Bonnefoy to say, 'Poetry is an increasing battle between representation and presence'. If so, then the translation of poetry is a battle of battles. The translation must know the source poem and take a distance from it, and in taking that distance allow a poem within or beyond the poem to be glimpsed – it must 'know well the two shores', as Anthony's translation has it. And yes, the two shores are the here and the beyond. A voice from afar inhabits a voice from here, uncannily. It's not a puzzle, it's magic, or divination, and Anthony is one those who can do it.

Stephen Romer

Our first meeting was I think at Bush House in the early '80s, then home to the BBC World Service, where in those days Tony earned his crust. I never learned what exactly he did there, for the more urgent business was always poetry, and the latest issue of the Menard Press. He was, instantly, a presence – lean, ardent, handsome. We met through our mutual friend Keith Bosley, the poet and translator, who also had a *gagne-pain* with Auntie, as a memorably basso profundo news announcer. We would talk poetry non-stop, while at intervals a red light would go on, giving warning that Keith would have to break off, to address the world. Our mutual interest in contemporary French poetry was central; how many times have I consulted that famous bright yellow special French issue of *Modern Poetry in Translation*, which Tony edited for Danny Weissbort! I still do, it seems to have a current running through it, like a magic vessel that keeps giving, a kind of manna, in the form of continued inspiration, a reminder of one's true direction. It is of course not the journal, but the man himself who over all these years has played that role for me. Our friendship was sealed when we discovered that we had, when students at Cambridge, each in his own epoch, taken down a random modern French poet from the shelf in a bookshop (Bowes & Bowes for him, Heffers for me) and found ourselves held in a magnetic force field. For him, Yves Bonnefoy, and for me, Jacques Dupin. But it was our mutual admiration (and friendship) for Bonnefoy that has been our ongoing 'joint project', culminating in the two-volume *Reader* (2018, 2020), which we co-edited for Carcanet with our friend John Naughton. More generally, I would simply say that Tony has for years been the steadfast go-to man, the first port of call, whenever one needed help with a translation, a quotation, a suggestion, an address. Or just a chat and a laugh. His acts of human kindness to me (frequently discreet, on one's behalf) have been numberless. And I know he has played that role for legions of us. Tony, vraiment, happy birthday, chapeau, et mille mercis.

Luís Amorim de Sousa

I heard his name from a poet. It could have been one of the many British and foreign poets who worked in Bush House, then the headquarters of the External Services of the BBC, where Tony worked. But it was Alberto de Lacerda, my closest friend and co-conspirator in matters of poetry finds and gallery forays, who asked me if I knew him: 'Anthony Rudolf. Tony. He is a poet, a translator, and a publisher as well. He is interested in Pessoa.'

Fernando Pessoa was then very poorly known in Britain. I took that as a very good reference. I asked Alberto in what department Tony worked. 'Oh! you will bump into him, I'm sure!' said Alberto.

And I did. In the newsroom. My purpose in being there had to do with updates on the revolution that had liberated Portugal from the Salazar regime. An unavoidable topic. But, unavoidably too, we were soon talking about poets and poetry. It made perfect sense to both of us.

Life intervened and it was many years later that I met Tony again. The scene was quite different: the Dulwich Art Gallery. The occasion was the inauguration of Paula Rego's exhibition of the Father Amaro set of paintings. Alberto, my wife Mary and I were there to celebrate Paula, our friend of many years. To my surprise Tony was there as her companion and model for Father Amaro. It was a happy moment for us all. And once again, Tony and I were sharing a common space. A space defined by our closeness to Paula.

My friendship with Tony widened from the world of poetry and progressive politics to include all that had to do with Paula. A friendship enhanced by the nobility of his selfless love for her, and his vocation for friendship.

I cannot end these words without a reference to the poet. Tony wrote many poems for Paula. His poem 'Pillar Box, Well Walk NW3' touched me especially. And once again, a shared place. Well Walk, facing a building deeply connected with me. A gentle wave to a window. And words of tenderness, closeness, the poetic side of life.

Peter Baldwin

I started my Delos Press imprint in 1987 with the publication of a revised version of Lawrence Durrell's 1963 play *An Irish Faustus*. I think that it was through meeting Durrell's contemporary, David Gascoyne (whom I also published), that I came to know Tony. David shared with me the addresses of two people who came to be very significant in my life – the Swiss poet Philippe Jaccottet (I published three books of his writings) and Tony Rudolf.

With our shared love of French poetry, there seemed to be an obvious synergy between Tony and me, and this proved to be most fruitful.

The first fruit was the chance for Delos to republish a very early work by Yves Bonnefoy, his 1946 *Traité du Pianiste*, a work 'born from the matrix of surrealism', to quote the book's cover blurb, in Tony's translation. This book had the happiest coincidence for me as Bonnefoy's friend Raymond Mason, best known as a sculptor but a very competent artist on the page, provided a frontispiece illustration; even though he had worked and lived in Paris since 1946, Raymond was born in my own native city, Birmingham.

A further collaboration involving Tony and me was the publication under my Delos Press imprint of a bilingual text *La Primauté du Regard / The Primacy of Gaze* (2000), a short collection of Bonnefoy's writings on Raymond Mason with Tony's translations of Bonnefoy's prose.

In 1999, I published Tony's own short poem 'Mandorla', and, the same year, Tony introduced me to Paula Rego's work when, with the support of her gallery, Marlborough, I published Ruth Rosengarten's essay on her: *Getting Away with Murder: Paula Rego and the Crime of Father Amaro*. Tony, who often sat for Paula, appears on the front cover of this book in one of her pastels from the Father Amaro series.

Tony is a man of great generosity – I only had to ask and a complimentary copy of a Menard Press book would be in my collection. Tony and Menard have been beacons to me, both as a publisher and as a reader. I salute him whole-heartedly.

Seeing, Again: Steven Jaron

Gabriel Josipovici suggested I see Anthony Rudolf as I was setting out from New York to Paris and Cairo to research my doctoral dissertation on Edmond Jabès. Our first meeting took place in the summer of 1994 at a garden party at Merton College. The occasion was a memorial gathering for his friend Peter Hoy, a fellow in French of the college and co-editor of *The Journals of Pierre Menard*, who had died a year earlier.

A single observation on Tony's editions of translations, poetry and essays stands out. It concerns self experience, a conception of which is defined in *Rescue Work: Memory and Text* (2001), his exploration of the futile yet imperative provocation of capturing the multifarious self's instability within the artifice of writing, as 'the construction or rescue of the ontological matrix of a self, an originative identity which shall enable the writer to write forwards even while living backwards'. I suggest that Tony's work as a writer and publisher may be considered as the strategic revision of self experience, a to-and-fro movement of renewal across time and space that cannot fully subjugate the transformations undergone, yet by necessity must occur. Thus the expansions from oral delivery to printed text, dedications, publisher's and translator's notes, prefaces and introductions, variations on a theme, asides and interpolations, appendices, afterwords and post-scripts, acknowledgements and biographical notices – each at times further annotated, some appearing (with different contents) more than once in a single publication or supplemented by a MenCard or an individual inscription.

Quicherat's *Thesaurus Poeticus Linguæ Latinæ* (1878) details how *revisere* signifies 'seeing again'. Tony is an exemplary practitioner of 'seeing, again' – the comma added in order to mark a caesura, which at once paradoxically divides and melds its different stages and angles of approach. 'Seeing, again', the anxiety-charged decisional process of revision, is by definition an incomplete achievement and so opens onto a future with all the possibilities that this implies.

Perhaps Tony's most important 'seeing, again' is that devoted to Jerzyk Feliks Urman, a child suicide in the terrors of the Churbn. The first version of his cousin's diary appeared in 1991; it was the object of 'seeing, again' in 2016. I can only describe the significance of this 'rescue work', which includes further testimony by Jerzyk's parents, as a fundamental contribution to the literature of loss in the face of wholesale atrocity.

Helen Tookey

The phone rings. A London number. I pick up, barely get out an initial 'Hello?' before the quick, keen voice breaks in: 'Helen? Tony. About the book – I've had an idea – '. And at the end of the call, he'll be off and away, suiting the action to the word, while I'm still halfway through saying goodbye.

When I first encountered Tony, via Carcanet, I was slightly disconcerted by this apparent abruptness. Later, as I got to know him better (and met him in non-telephonic real life), I came to enjoy it, to connect it to the sheer drive and energy that characterise Tony's way of being in the world – and that have powered his work as writer, translator, publisher, mentor and facilitator and creative friend to so many people.

I had the pleasure and privilege of working with Tony on *European Hours*, his collected poems, which Carcanet published in 2017. Re-reading the book, I'm struck again by the richness and range of its conversations – with paintings, books, music, cities; with history, memory, friendship, love. The book came at the same time as the (for me, distressing and dismaying) Brexit vote, and I remember it felt like a talisman, a book of hours speaking an unshakeable faith in connection, and especially in the power of art (in the widest sense) to reach across borders, across space and time.

A vital presence in *European Hours* was, is, that of Tony's long-time partner, the painter Paula Rego; from the cover painting onwards (Tony modelling for one of Paula's series of paintings inspired by the nineteenth-century Portuguese novel *The Crime of Father Amaro*), the book stands as tribute to their relationship. I love the poem 'Colombine at the Picasso Exhibition, Paris, November 1996', with its opening lines 'She leaves me at the photographs / to reapply / herself to the paintings', its punning depiction of Rego as both loved companion and working artist: 'I observe / how well she looks // at what / is seen'. I hope too that Tony's fascinating and moving reflections on modelling for Paula, and on the hours spent in the uniquely intimate (yet working) space of her studio, will be published and will find the readers they deserve.

In the short prose piece 'Old Wyldes', published as an appendix to *European Hours*, Tony mused: 'I'm now over seventy: shall I find the time to read the Dickens novels I've not yet read? If so, what will become of my project to reread Dostoevsky? There is no time to lose'. I don't know how the Dickens (or the Dostoevsky) may be coming along, but, Tony, here's to many more years, and *all* the projects.

C.K. Stead

When Anthony Rudolf came to New Zealand in 2011 he got in touch with me (Carcanet was the connection) with the idea that I might take him to Waikumete Cemetery to find the grave of the celebrated German Jewish poet Karl Wolfskehl. Wolfskehl had escaped from the Nazis in the 1930s and spent the remainder of his life in Auckland, where he died in 1948. Tony and I made that visit successfully and he came to dinner that evening, where we discovered we had been in the same room together a number of years before, a London University occasion when Tony had presented his translation of Balzac's 'Gillette' or 'Le chez d'ouevre inconnu' together with his theory that the story, about a painting the artist had spent so much time on that it had been, so to speak, painted to death and become incomprehensible, was in fact Balzac's prediction of the non-figurative art of the future. I'd had an entirely different reading of the story, but that hardly mattered. Our friendship was to be through books, reading and literature in translation, and would continue and develop, mostly at a distance via email, but sometimes when one or the other was on a visit – I there, or he here in New Zealand, where he has family connections.

Tony and I exchanged poems and fictions, and I discovered in him a reader of such range I was always both impressed and faintly daunted by it. It was during these years that he published his collected poems, *European Hours*, and his extraordinary literary-autobiography *Silent Conversations*, seven hundred pages of critical reflection on a life of reading. Over these years I have also caught up with some of his earlier publications, not only his translations from the French (Vigée and Bonnefoy), but also *The Arithmetic of Memory*. I met his partner, the painter Paula Rego (whose favoured male model he has been), visited her astonishing studio and, not far away, his apartment (the one his most recent publication gave us a tour of); have dined with them in their favoured Camden Town restaurant, and enjoyed the warmth and sparkle of their company.

Tony Rudolf is a remarkable and civilised poet, publisher and man of letters, and it has been my great good luck to be numbered among his friends.

Frederic Raphael

Anthony Rudolf's *Silent Conversations*, which testifies to his long devotion, as writer and publisher, to literature and the witness it can bear to the noblest and foulest of human aspirations, received scant attention from English critics. It is tempting to attribute this to malice; laziness is more probable. While leavened with touches of self-deprecation, Rudolf's work has been compiled with daunting seriousness. 'My book... involves excess, desire and the controlling hand of absolute possession... Subject matter and form are dialectically interrelated, and out of the interrelationship is born... the love child of conscious and unconscious longings for healing and wholeness, for unity and redemption...' Not many laughs there, you might say, but no affectations of self-importance, no parade of *m'as-tu-vu?* ostentation. In person Tony (let's call him) has a self-deprecating humour which never makes light of the horror, the horror, of Jewish life in Europe's twentieth century, but turns his company into a delightful reminder that light-heartedness had better have its place in the life and work of the eminently serious man.

Anne Sere & Mark Hutchinson

Every day he steps down from a painting hung on the wall of a big museum or tumbles quietly from the pages of a book housed in a gigantic library and goes out into the world. The people he meets are entranced by his most unusual presence and glance round as he passes, wondering who is this figure they have seen and read about, who reminds them of a scene in a painting or a beautifully written story. It's Anthony Rudolf, one might say, born eighty years ago and as comfortable in French or English as he is in Hebrew, and no doubt in Iroquois, too. Whereupon everyone tries to recall the poem or novel in which they first read about this Anthony, the painting in which they first saw his face or silhouette or suit-and-tie forever. No doubt there's a sixteenth-century novella telling the story of his devoted, chivalrous, passionate love for a beautiful Portuguese lady who painted wonderful pictures in which he also appears. And there's definitely a Borges tale where he weaves in and out at the flick of a wand, moving elegantly back and forth through space and time like a man who can walk through walls. In that film of Proust descending the steps of the Église de la Madeleine in Paris, he's there on the steps, of course, at Marcel's side. And observe how, in Shakespeare, he glides airily about the stage, helping out other members of the cast with his customary air of gravity and amusement. In the same way that he crosses the Channel from London to Paris, or Paris to London via Lisbon, Tony, as his friends call him – though Anthony Rudolf is a delightful name, the title of a novel no less, with two first names facing one another – travels about in the books and paintings where he truly belongs and feels most at home. To count among one's friends a creature with a gift as rare as this is a blessing indeed.

Marina Warner

Anthony began posing for Paula Rego because, he realised, it was the only way he could spend time with her, as she was never out of the studio, never not working. Around twenty years ago, I was putting together a show for the Science Museum about Metamorphosis – and wanted to include a work of Paula's because she is a preeminent artist of shapeshifting fantasies. I suggested Ovid as inspiration; she proposed Kafka's Gregor Samsa instead. The eventual drawings and paintings show Anthony naked, on his back, with his arms and legs waving in the air, and looking out at the viewer with terrified eyes, in torment at his transformation. It's an image of bewilderment and pathos, and a very very tough pose to hold – Anthony's arms and legs had to be held up to the ceiling on a cradle of ropes.

Kafka has long haunted Anthony; you could say he's his model, his forebear: the European range, the passionate reading, the mordant humour, the brooding and tenacity. 'Kafka's Doll' is one of my most favourite writings of Anthony's, in which he takes a passing anecdote from the writer's life and turns it into a bittersweet wisdom tale that, incidentally, gives a very different perspective on Kafka himself: Kafka meets a little girl in the park who is distraught because she has lost her doll; the writer then composes a letter to her from the doll, telling her not to worry, she has only gone away on holiday and is having a lovely time. The little girl dries her tears, and soon afterwards, forgets all about the doll.

The tale also builds on the possibility that the world of pure imagination exists – somewhere. That is an aspect of Rego's portrait of Anthony as Gregor the beetle, and it connects for me to many imaginary worlds that Anthony and Paula shared. *Favourite Poems* is a booklet Anthony had privately printed for Paula in the last months of her life. It includes Keats's 'Ode to a Nightingale', Coleridge's 'Kubla Khan' and verses from Rossetti's 'Goblin Market'. Yearning for an elsewhere made palpable by poetic vision, be it Xanadu or the lost home of Auden's 'Refugee Blues', provides a common thread, always tugged at by the melancholy knowledge beneath that 'fancy… deceiving elf' is at work, the powerful maker of this refuge, the refuge of art.

Gabriel Josipovici

Tony,
Thank you for encouraging me to plunge into writing about Kafka all those years ago when you guest-edited an issue of *European Judaism* devoted to him and his work; thank you for publishing four stories of mine together as a slim but coherent volume for the Menard Press; thank you for the wonderful obituary you wrote of my mother for the *Guardian*; and thank you for your constant encouragement as both friend and publisher. The selfless work you have done promoting authors you believed in, bringing Jewish and French authors in particular to the attention of an ever more insular British public, has been a wonder to behold. May your warm and enthusiastic presence permeate our culture for a long time to come.

Ifigenija Simonović

Anthony,
Didn't you notice me at the Poetry Society in the year 1978? Didn't you publish my collection of poems twenty years later? Didn't you invite me to a bar at Bloomsbury and tell me about Virginia Woolf, prompting me to learn more? Didn't you tell me about Rebecca West and Jean Rhys and Stevie Smith, about poets of the First World War? Didn't you take me to East London and show me old, deserted synagogues? Didn't you become my first and only 'regular customer' at Covent Garden? Didn't you order a tea pot for your son's wedding and didn't I feel terrible charging for it so that you would not be offended? Didn't you tell me about men and women in portraits at the National Gallery, old and new? Didn't you show me Ophelia at the Tate Gallery? Didn't you tell me all I know about Jewish poetry, before, during, after the Holocaust? Didn't you take me to the Freud Museum and opened a new field of learning for me? Didn't you introduce me to the British Library and to R.B. Kitaj? Didn't you introduce me to Paula Rego? Didn't you come to the Royal Academy, where I was a ticket seller, and allow me to give you a complimentary ticket, the only thing of any value that I was able to give you?

Anthony, isn't there more and more and more! There is no word huge enough to express my gratitude.

For your birthday I wish you many happy returns and I promise to come and visit you soon.

Yours eternally, Ifigenija

Elte Rauch

Dear Anthony,
Sometimes in life you meet people, you feel drawn to them, and you don't know why. It is as if they carry a secret, yet to be revealed. You share differences. You agree to disagree. You treat each other with respect. You lose contact, only to find one another years later in different circumstances. The reason why becomes clearer, with hindsight. As Wallace Stevens, one of your favourite poets, expressed it:

These are not things transformed.
Yet we are shaken by them as if they were.
We reason about them with a later reason.

My thoughts go back to how we met, to your nephew Jesse, and to his mother, your sister Annie. The one I lived with in Bristol as a student, the other introduced you and me to each other.

It was evident from the start that we had much in common, and we still are continuing the conversation we started then, right to this day. But the secret was revealed only later. Not when we first met. It was shortly after I turned forty, because by then I had started my own publishing house.

As the years passed, and with those years our conversations and correspondence, you have truly become a best friend. We are kindred souls with similar minds, and through our love of literature, translating and publishing we are always in touch, despite the distance in years and miles between us.

And this year you have permitted me to merge my Amsterdam based HetMoet Press with your respected and much loved Menard Press. Henceforth, our friendship and our great passion is nobly 'embodied'... and you have enabled me to establish a UK imprint! Perhaps we could call it a *Mysterium Coniunctionis*.

The true mystery of connection is the synthesis of differences. With your eighty years, we are perhaps not so much a difference as a summation. A sum that can be divided, apportioned, and shared. Shared with a new generation of readers!

And so it is. Connections carry promises that are only to be reasoned about 'with a later reason'.

Happy Birthday Anthony.

Thank you.

Tony of the Undersea: Gregory O'Brien

I haven't seen Anthony Rudolf for ten years – not since we said our farewells at St Pancras, having just disembarked from the Paris–London express. We had spent three elevating, energising days in the French capital, during which Tony had been the most gracious yet incisive of tour guides. The excursion had its genesis in things we had been discussing.

At Tony's instigation, a couple of years earlier, I had corresponded with Yves Bonnefoy while working on a book about the Australian/New Zealand painter Euan Macleod. The walking, totemic figure central to Giacometti's art – and eloquently chronicled in Bonnefoy's monograph – had been given an antipodean reprise in Macleod's figure paintings. This was something I set to exploring further. In due course, Tony spent a productive hour with Euan Macleod and me going through the storeroom of the Museum of New Zealand Te Papa Tongarewa in Wellington, losing ourselves among their McCahons, Woollastons and Macleods. We were expecting to see more of Tony in this part of the world in the years that followed, but Paula Rego's health and then the pandemic put paid to that.

In Paris, February 2012, Yves Bonnefoy took us out to a restaurant titled – appropriately given the poetic nature of the company – 'Basho', a stroll from his home in Montmartre. The following day, with Yves, we visited Paula Rego's exhibition at the Portuguese cultural centre. In a photograph I took on my phone of Tony and Yves, both look satisfied and Yves is, I would say, pleasurably ruffled by Rego's uncompromising, exemplary works. No one needed to be converted.

The next morning, Tony and I swam through Monet's waterlily room in the Orangerie before lunching just across from the Gare du Nord with a friend of mine I thought Tony should meet: Pierre Furlan, a fiction writer and translator of Janet Frame and Tony's old friend Paul Auster, amongst others. The literary world is a village – possibly an Eastern European one, and quite probably a Jewish one, in this instance.

Such an anarchic yet endlessly interconnected global village seems to be a central premise of Tony's compendium of a lifetime's reading, *Silent Conversations*. Therein he offers us a 360-degree view of the world of letters from his not-too-elevated seat in the village square.

Although our paths haven't crossed in the past decade, by way of *Silent Conversations*, it feels as if he has had a seat at our table the whole time. In that book too, Tony configures as a kind of travel companion or tour guide, *sans* umbrella, to regions known and unknown. Thinking of Tony now, my mind fixes him in the seat beside me on the Eurostar, mid-way through the rail tunnel under the English Channel. Sited accordingly in the undersea, he reminds me of Jules Verne's Captain Nemo, whose submarine *Nautilus* contained a library of some 12,000 titles. In Tony's case, however, the man himself is the library. And *Silent Conversations*, which appeared a couple of years after our Paris trip, presented as an outward projection of that well-stocked mind, with its intricate shelving and cross-referencing.

Riding the tidal surge above us, I imagine the English Channel's freight of container ships and refugee-boats, fishing vessels and fish. I also recognise, up above us, the curved planks of Yves Bonnefoy's poetic vessels, of 'Beckett's Dinghy'... Maybe the water has Monet-ish tonings and even some lilies or their saltwater equivalents...

And maybe this is the exact place on the planet where Tony is most at home – midway between England and Europe, in motion, shuttling to and fro. So much of his life's thinking and energy has gone into bringing those catchments into a brisk, mutually energising and enriching proximity. Tony's collected poems, *European Hours*, also straddles the United Kingdom and the European Union. All of his writing is a paean to the interesting, boisterous, challenging and necessary comings-together of different cultures, with bearings taken from Paula Rego and Walter Benjamin as they are from Ruskin and Auden. His life's work is a passionate argument against the narrowing of culture. Brexit must have hurt him. It must still hurt. But the clock only goes forward.

Year

STANLEY MOSS

What are years? In early Chinese waters
there was a monster named *Year*, she came
to harass womankind and mankind at a fixed date
at the beginning of Spring. Later a wise man
taught people to explode fireworks to scare
the monster away. It became the custom
to explode fireworks on New Year's Day.
Now there is a frightened monster, nothing like
a dragon that brings good luck to the worthy.
I don't have words to say what *Year* looks like.
Yes, *Year* has eyes of many colours, donkey ears
for music, webbed warrior feet, an anus
for disapproved holidays.
Year holds public property that is not hers.

In short, to the God fearing, *Year* looks like history,
has several deceiving eyes. Still, for a month's sake,
Year modestly hides in the forest and in kind waters.
Years are rare. A few of us believe
Year has children. I think there is a continuing.

Born in Winter, there are premature years.
Forest fires are incubators.
There are so many wildfires in California,
Mother Year and *Father Year* often made love
under sequoias. It's a long swim for *Year*
from San Francisco Bay to Shanghai.
Year rests in Hawaii. Twenty summers ago,
Year swam in the Grand Canal to the Biennale,
her tail splashing laughter at the biannual
that had nothing to do with *Year*.
What did opinionated paintings, painted for beauty
and money, have to do with the monster?
No one painted mortality, eternity for nothing.

A happy few saw *Year* on Loch Lomond's bonnie
    banks.
An Irishman near the Sligo told me in a pub
he saw *Year* fighting with a minute,
and minute won. Dead drunk, I told him

when I swim in the Hudson River,
backstroke, freestyle, and kicking
with my one good leg, sooner or later
I know *Year* will devour me. Till then,
I molest *Year* in Januarys, try to capture her.

Year understands languages. All languages,
including Chinese, have ancient African roots.
There are 46 Aboriginal dialects in Mexico alone.
Year survived the 1520 genocide in Mexico.
Year after year, she is amused
at the toast in Polish, 'A hundred *years*'.

Year struggles, aristocratic Time says
'*Year* has a Cockney accent.'
The loneliest fisherman in the world,
I try to spearfish an extra *Year* for me,
as if it were a whale.
There are *Years* of many colours,
black, white, purple, green *Years*.
I don't forget a *Year* that looked like a sparrow,
flew like an eagle. She flies forever like some
waterbirds, never touching water.
Year is a clean word, a bullet shot
in the temple of the head.
Forever and *always* are dirty words.
'Words have no word for words that are not true.'

Year holds open his or her mouth,
fills it with ocean and spits Time in my face.
Year spits salty Kosher wrinkles on my face.
I don't lie, I write on the way to Truth so you
believe what I say. *Year* isn't a metaphor, or
a Bible story. I laugh and say, 'Leap year is not
an extra day in February, or a leap over
a tennis net of days.' I don't want to waste words.

I kiss *Year* the monster with her many tongues,
I make good use of my tongue that is guilty and
    innocent.

The Wasp Trap

A.E. STALLINGS

High Groves Estate Villa, Old Epidaurus

for Andrew and Rebecca

Wasps besieged the gentle company,
Dive-bombing the cheese board, troubling
Our gestures, walking the thin rims of gin-
And-tonic glasses. Waving them away
The host was stung. Was it a kind of sin

To clear the air? We spoke of pollinators,
The wasp-death at the heart of purple figs.
Poison-squeamish, I proposed a trap,
Scissored off the top of a plastic bottle,
Inverted it inside the base, no cap,

And glugged a sugary liquid through the funnel
To lure them to the bottom: quinine-laced
Tonic water, the dregs of orange-ade.
The descent is broad and easy down the tunnel,
But getting out, as Virgil might have said,

Is tricky. We saw one creep in, then pop
Out through the bottle's mouth, into a lake
Of pleasure. In our ad-hoc panopticon,
Searching for the narrow escape, it drowned.
Our conversation paused, as one by one

Wasps found themselves perplexed, as in the plush
Labyrinth of a young fig's involute
Inflorescence. The air was bright and wingless
Awash in afternoon, the opposing hill
Darkening. Did the cicadas seem to sing less?

In between the day and night, the yammers
Of golden jackals rose, not dog nor wolf,
A fringe of wilderness. Soon bats would skim
The turquoise lozenge of the swimming pool
Just above the tipsy midnight swimmers,

Swooping on the light-ensorcelled moths,
While the distant headlights of the stars
Would wink and trundle on their ancient gears,
Letting the odd meteors come sliding
Across the windshield of the sky like tears.

The day diminishes, it's late, and yet
Must we not savor this doomed beauty? Friends
Gathered up this once from the earth's ends
Spoke of Arian heresy, the tower
Not far from here, long tumbled down, the hour

Rosy and sweet as a ripe cut-open fig.
What could we do but toast it with rosé,
And watch the wasps' short struggles against long odds
In that disposable transparency,
Contented as a counsel of the gods?

Three Poems

AUDREY HENDERSON

Requiring Wings

This was the zenith of the day – west wind, rent clouds over the hills, the roar
of air and leaves, stupefaction of the drought-stricken land after rainfall,
the grass eager to be green, even in October. Some cars drive by, early
afternoon, raw sunlight, all of it laying stunned, like flesh under a ripped-off
Band-Aid. I am the soggy flesh puckered and tender. Does the season change
or does the North just find us again. I had never not known freedom, and what
I now know is that freedom contains fancy, a zephyr of thought, that passes
through the room, skimming our heads on the way, and an important element
of fancy is motion. Fancy is going somewhere; contains possibility, chance,
delight. The permanent wasps on our storm window buzz briefly, they walk
most of the time, sniffing the aluminum, but out of some kind of boredom maybe,
they buzz, requiring wings. When you are raised clinging to a *drum*, a backbone
of earth, when your first geology is raised above a panorama, then the wind threatens
to detach, the light annihilate. I try to start, I try to start again and the lack of air,
the lack of the zephyr, the day's bee-flower, its scent, well, it isn't there.

Salamanders

A wood, a pond, waterfowls at the far end, distinguishable,
moving and not rocks. Up here, an old road where the waters
have pooled. No carts pass nowadays and thawed snow burst
the ditches to lull, full of spawn, tan silt. On spring nights
they sing, in the star waters, emerging slippery, all at once.
They know the time has come to enter webbed darkness.
It is peaceable and amniotic in the pool, white leaves fall.
And the track wends through bedrock, sweet light, yellow
violets. A horse-shoe hangs by a cellar hole – stone, cut
expertly once, now moss-silent and deeper than the height
of a man who brought tools rattling in a wooden cart to make
a cellar out of wilderness and someone in a cart came by,
lantern swinging in the rain, late one night, stayed all night.

National Gallery of Scotland

It's a small detail, maybe only three of us
know. When I come to look at it, I feel
you and Vincent standing there. Artists
are always hiding secrets in plain sight.
Sitting now, I can attest that no-one has
stood before it long enough to find him,
almost invisible among the plum petals.
Still no-one has got close. Yesterday on
the train, a horse, some trees sped past
in a blur and then the fields were there
a moment longer. The hills seemed almost
permanent, which got me thinking about
deep behind, blue hills that never ever move.

Two Poems

JODIE HOLLANDER

Dream #2

New York

She's living in a dingy little apartment
   with a dusty old couch, a sagging bed;
rats scurry through the old floorboards;
   crumbs are all over the kitchen table.
Yet my Mother seems happy in this place,
   she's humming as she zips up her dress,
fluffs her hair, spritzes on perfume.
   Tonight she's going out to hear a concert
with a sleazy man with slicked-back hair.
   He's at the door now, already bragging,
claiming to know the star violinist.
   My mother's nodding, smiling agreeably;
she practically floats out the door with him.
   I follow the two of them into the darkness;
I watch them holding hands, chatting away,
   suddenly it hits me: he will hurt her.
He'll take her back to that dirty little flat,
   rip off her dress, pin her body down,
cover her mouth; no one will ever hear her;
   only the rats will know what this man did.
Maybe I can help her, I can stop this –
   I'll hide behind this building and I'll wait,
then I'll beat this motherfucker to the ground.
   The concert's over, my adrenaline is pumping,
they turn the corner walking hip to hip,
   and I punch the bad man as hard as I can.
But something's wrong, my little arm is broken,
   and instead of punching him he punches me,
and he takes my mother with him into the night.
   This isn't fair, I'm just a little girl,
I want to scream. I can't make a sound –
   I lie very still, beneath a heavy sky
the darkness is so thick I can't see
   my bloody kid teeth, scattered on the pavement.

Dream #4

Breaking In

When I break into storybook white houses,
   it's always cool inside from air conditioning,
and smells of fabric softener and dryer sheets.
   Often, I just stand there in the darkness,
thinking, *I should really not be here* –
   But I can't seem to help myself from breaking
the lamps, the vases, all the pretty china,
   the glossy family pictures in their frames.
Nor can I help destroying the parents' room:
   tossing the lingerie from the drawers,
sticking a knife into the frilly pillows.
   And yet the nursery is always the worst:
the matching beds lined with stuffed toys,
   a nightstand with a copy of *Goodnight Moon*.
To think, parents reading to their darlings,
   kissing their little foreheads, tucking them in,
saying *I love you*, and turning off the lights –
   Now I'm sobbing, heading to the kitchen,
rifling through the cupboard looking for food:
   I start stuffing crackers in my mouth,
I'm eating them so fast, I think I'll choke –
   'till I hear someone's keys jangling:
A mother and a father, speaking to each other,
   I dart into the bathroom, hide inside the tub.
I've been here a million times before,
   I used to hide in the bathtub as a girl,
and wish to disappear down the drain.
   I hear the doorknob slowly start to turn:
I wonder, will they call the cops on me,
   perhaps they'll pity me and let me stay;
what if they love me, even want to adopt me?
   Now the bathroom door is creaking open,
and I don't know if I'm a kid or thirty-eight –
   but I feel my body suddenly go cold.

'We Should All Calm Down'

Robert Crawford, *Eliot After 'The Waste Land'* (Jonathan Cape) £25

CRAIG RAINE

If you want the precise configuration of the Porters' Lodge at Merton College, Robert Crawford is your man: 'Entering Merton College through its fifteenth-century gatehouse surmounted by relief sculptures of Bishop Walter de Merton, St John the Baptist and other religious figures was like stepping into a monastery. Its hefty wooden gate led through a stone archway past a porter's lodge where a college servant kept a suspicious watch on all incomers...' (*Young Eliot*). But perhaps you are anxious to know about Claremont railroad depot at 6.20 a.m. on Thursday 29 December [1932]: 'oddly Spanish baroque concrete frontage and cruciform doors made it look part train station, part church'. T.S. Eliot was met there by Emily Hale, with whom he had been unrequitedly in love since 1914 – in spite of marrying Vivien Haigh-Wood in June 1915. In 1932, Emily's inclinations were not fully disclosed. But obviously you will first want to know that Claremont's population 'numbered under 3,000' and that the campus grounds of Scripps College were still being developed by the irresistibly named landscape architect Edward Huntsman-Trout.

One of the problems of this biography is length. This second volume, *Eliot After 'The Waste Land'*, is 609 pages long and covers the years from 1922 to Eliot's death in January 1965. Quite long enough, you might think, after reading it. A typical volume of Eliot's letters covers three years and takes just over a thousand pages, with impeccably informative and unstinting annotation by John Haffenden. That 8,357 page project has reached Volume 9, to the end of 1941. Robert Crawford has an impossible task, made more difficult by his determination to cram in everything, or nearly everything. Do we need the detail that Eliot's secretary, Miss Bradby [Anne Ridler] observed that 'when afternoon tea was served he did not take the sugar; Miss Bradby noticed how he "would carefully remove the teaspoon from his saucer before it became slopped with tea"'. Now you know. We could perhaps have dispensed with Huntsman-Trout. His inclusion and the inclusion of similar bit parts – who cares about Mrs Aubrey Coker of Bicester, the sister of Hope Mirrlees? – creates fatal expository compression elsewhere.

An illustration: a Faber Book Committee discussed swear-words in Auden's *The Orators*. This is Crawford muffing it: 'Rather than risking prosecution over the expression '*A fucked hen*', Tom suggested Auden might substitute '*A June Bride*' – 'sore but satisfied' was Tom's explanation.' John Haffenden's fuller footnote, in summary, tells us that, in 1965, Auden remembered '[he] had used [in *The Orators*] the phrase *A fucked hen*. In 1932 publishers still boggled at the four-letter words and a substitute had to be found.' Eliot suggested *A June Bride.* Auden was initially baffled that this should be thought to be equivalent. Eliot explained that in an election, the defeated candidate, asked about the voting figures, said he felt like a June bride: 'sore but satisfied'. The victor was also asked how he felt about the voting figures: 'like a June bride,' he returned, 'I knew it would be big, but I didn't think it would be that big.' In 1965, this anecdote was suppressed to spare Valerie Eliot's feelings. But Humphrey Carpenter retailed it in his 1981 biography of Auden and the robust Mrs Eliot wrote to him: 'The anecdote about TSE and the June bride is delicious!'

Everything in Crawford is cramped, trimmed, impacted, truncated, impeded. You can't see the wood for the sawdust. The reader picks through narrative lumber, sorts through an unselective clutter. For example, consider this ungainly centaur of a sentence: 'In the same month Tom further advanced his slow-moving process of becoming a British subject by signing a formal declaration of his wishes, and grew eager to write about Baudelaire, another abiding preoccupation...' The connection? Same month, same sentence?

It isn't all stock cubes – the correspondence reduced to dense, indigestible hard-tack. Crawford has disenchanted things to say about the early days of the Faber poetry list. He has also discovered some valuable new material: Aurelia Bolliger's archival deposit at Bryn Mawr. Aurelia Bolliger was the American partner of the poet Ralph Hodgson ('How delightful to meet Mr Hodgson! / (Everyone wants to know *him*.') The Eliots liked the couple (and their dog, Pickwick), ignored their irregular relationship, and became for a time quite intimate. Aurelia sometimes stayed the night. Her memoirs cast intermittent light on marital mysteries. A letter written in extremis by the mad Vivien begs Eliot from her nursing home (2 November 1925): 'Please write to this doctor instantly and tell him the truth, that we have had sexual relations. // Do these things for me. Especially about our married life and make him see it *had* been good. All here believe not. Also explain about the scars on my back.' Bolliger saw the scars and thought they looked 'like measles' and might have been caused by injections.

Her comments on the Eliots' sex life, though, are actually secondhand gossip from Ottoline Morrell: 'Eliot is not very vital'; Vivien is 'sexually dissatisfied'; Vivien has 'carried on a kind of love affair here with B Russell'. Only the last of these speculations has any weight, because Ottoline herself had a kind of love affair with Russell. The tittle-tattle of outsiders is intrinsically unreliable. The principals themselves might not be entirely clear. This is Henry Ware Eliot on marriage (12 June 1925). He is announcing his engagement to Theresa Garrett: 'One goes to a bourne of which no traveller ever tells. It is the most secret of all secret cults.'

Eliot's sex life. What a goad to invention. Von Humboldt Fleisher in Bellow's novel, *Humboldt's Gift*, is a marker: 'Approved by T S Eliot (about whom, when he was off his nut, he would spread the most lurid improbable sexual scandal)'. The opacity of marriage. We can't be certain. But that is no bar to the biographer. In his first volume, Crawford had this to say about Vivien's nickname for Eliot 'My dearest Wonkypenky': '"Wonky" is English slang for "faulty", and, though the word is not in the *Oxford English Dictionary* (which lists only the verb to "penk", meaning to throb), it seems clear "penky" is slang for penis.' So far, so unlikely. Crawford's conclusion: 'So the letter, anxious and affectionate, also hints that Vivien was used to Tom having physical problems: "wonkypenky" surely implies a difficulty in sexual performance.' Breathtakingly unjustified. 'Wonky' means 'out of true' and it isn't certain that 'penky' means penis. It *might* mean that Eliot's penis was not straightforward, but had a Bill Clinton curve. It may simply be affectionate nonsense. What it can't be is a wife crass enough to address her husband *affectionately* as Faulty Penis.

This is of a piece with Crawford's conviction that Eliot's favourite lines from the *Purgatorio* demonstrate that Eliot had 'a long-lasting association of sexual desire with sin' – because they are spoken by Arnaut Daniel, who is in Purgatory doing penance for lust. This is *evidence*? So, on the one hand, Eliot is sexually incompetent, damaged goods, with a low sex-drive. On the other hand, driven by sinful lust, like Arnaut Daniel.

In Crawford's first volume, Eliot's straightforward admission to Geoffrey Faber that he had committed adultery was massaged away: in its place, flirtations, 'emotionally dependent friendships with women', imaginary adultery 'in his heart'. The biographer tending to the common prejudice that Eliot wasn't much of a tail-chaser. True, Virginia Woolf wished Tom 'had more spunk in him'. And Amos, the African-American chauffeur, graduate of Howard University and poetry reader, in Chandler's *The Long Goodbye* says, 'the guy didn't know very much about women'. Crawford has changed his mind. He now thinks that adultery was committed with Nancy Cunard – because he has subsequently read Eliot's more amplified, circumstantial admission of adultery to Emily Hale. However, Eliot never names Nancy Cunard and her memoirs only admit to a strong attraction to Eliot but nowhere claim adultery took place. No amount of peripheral detail pressed into service – her emerald and gold interior decoration, her knowing *The Duchess of Malfi* by heart – can shore up the claim, can clinch the adulterous clinch. Plausibility isn't fact, though it rapidly becomes so here: 'the tormented husband of Vivien, adulterous lover of Nancy Cunard...'

From October 1930 to October 1957, Eliot wrote continuously and secretly to Emily Hale in America. (His side of the correspondence, over a million words, was unveiled at Princeton in January 2020, and will be published online at the end of the year on tseliot.com.) His letters were at first amorous, Auden's 'baltering torrent'. They sank to a 'soodling thread' after the death of Vivi-

en Eliot, when Eliot realised that he no longer loved Emily enough to marry her – and rescinded his promise. The Emily Hale correspondence is a game-changer. It shows Eliot without his social mask, determined to leave behind a true, unvarnished record of his life for posterity – 'emerods', bad teeth, dentures and all. He envisages a corrective: 'There will be as much in existence to give a very false impression of me, and so few clues to the truth. Can I make clear to you my feeling, I wonder. I admit that it is egoistic and perhaps selfish; but is it not natural, when one has had to live in a mask all one's life, to be able to hope that some day people can know the truth, if they want it.' The Hale correspondence is a diary, more so as it progresses, as well as a set of love letters. Eliot encloses letters he has received from other writers – Joyce, Virginia Woolf – to record his life as lived: 'It does canker to feel that so long as there is any interest in me at all, if there is, my life and work will be misunderstood to the end of time.'

No more credence is given to Carole Seymour-Jones's reckless speculations in *The Painted Shadow: A Life of Vivienne Eliot* (2001) – the covert homosexual careerist cynically pimping his wife to Bertrand Russell. Instead, we have Eliot tactfully, considerately rejecting an advance from Lytton Strachey and telling Emily Hale, from personal experience, confidently and calmly, that mild homoerotic feelings for one's pupils are perfectly natural and harmless. His tone is sane, humorous, frank and far from the cold but tortured figure of legend. The relationship between Eliot and Emily Hale, as it develops, involves quite a lot of kissing and physical contact, but it is celibate. Crawford's impertinent forays into psychoanalysis aren't persuasive: 'Did Emily see something of her poet-priest father in Tom? Conscious of sexual immaturity, did Tom seek a lover or a surrogate mother?' What is the evidence that Eliot was sexually immature, a man unable to get out of his famous four piece suit into his birthday suit? Surely not his adulterous affair with the rackety Nancy Cunard?

The other significant addition to the Eliot sex narrative is Eliot's weekly letters to his second wife, Valerie. Crawford is a mite prim about them. They sit rather uneasily with the accepted profile of a sexually-disgusted, sexually-timorous, sexually-ineffectual Eliot. On the contrary, he is sexually happy – in the delicious dirty way people are sexually happy. What Kipling, in his story 'Wireless', calls 'the naked soul's confession of its physical yearning for its beloved – unclean as we count uncleanliness; unwholesome, but human exceedingly'. Crawford shies away from the naturally indecent desires and the occasional intimate setbacks normal in any sexual relationship. These letters are a very human document – *hypocrite lecteur, mon semblable, mon frère* – a mirror in which we can recognise our own sexual selves in private, exalted and embarrassing in equal measure. Ultimately, they constitute a caution against the reflex condescension brought to bear on Eliot's earlier sexual life. Wittgenstein applies here: whereof we cannot speak, thereof we must be silent.

In Volume 9 of Eliot's Letters, on at least four occasions, Eliot approves the idea of John Hayward accumulating a quasi-documentary equivalent of Proust – a novel called *Beechingstoke* 'that was to be a re-creation of the social and literary world of London in the thirties'. In sum, Hayward's 'mon recherche du temps perdu'. Eliot was 'an encouraging but impatient taskmaster', Haffenden tells us. This chimes with Eliot's concern to leave a proper record of his life's contours and authentic textures in his correspondence with Emily Hale. But there are concurrent objections. He writes to Hayward: 'if I could destroy every letter I have ever written in my life I would do so before I die. I should like to leave as little biography as possible'. And of course, in the end, Eliot repudiated the record contained in his letters to Emily Hale.

These are interesting contradictions, opposed opinions seriously held, and I wonder if they don't shed oblique light on the instances of anti-Semitism in the Emily Hale correspondence. We are familiar with contradiction when we consider feelings. That love and hate are imbricated is a staple of psychoanalysis. But I think opinions are often more ductile, more emotional than we imagine in our pursuit of logic and clarity. Henry James puts it well in *The Bostonians* when he has Verena Tarrant glide over 'the many traps that life sets for our consistency'.

Think of Catherine Sloper in *Washington Square*: at the denouement, she refuses to marry Morris Townsend, knowing him to be a mercenary bounder. But she still loves him – and 'averted herself rigidly from the idea of marrying other people'. James lists her entirely acceptable, worthy but disappointed suitors. His unique novelistic insight is that we live in contradiction, existing habitually on both sides of the fracture. In theory at least, in his preface to Volume 2, Crawford agrees: 'I try to present Tom Eliot's life and work without undue moralizing... my aim is not to neaten his life, or reduce it to one expository template, but to let it emerge in its sometimes complex, contradictory messiness.' In fact, he does moralise on occasion. In Volume 1, though, he was more categorical: 'I do not attempt to disguise anti-Semitic moments in his work, or other elements of racism and sexism deeply ingrained in his society and never fully outgrown.' The difference in emphasis between the volumes is, I think, the result of reading Eliot's letters to Emily Hale and the emergence of positive evidence about Eliot and Jews.

Crawford reports that in 1947, the Jewish poet Edward Field accused Eliot of anti-Semitism. Eliot's answer was defiant and downright: 'I am afraid that you are over-sensitive and like some other people inclined to find anti-Semitism wherever the word Jew is used in connection with an individual who is not depicted as one of the finest types of his people. There is no anti-Semitism in my poetry whatever.' In other words, not all characters are to be taken as generic representatives. Crawford finds Eliot's tone deplorable, cold, a failure of empathy, given the recent Nazi horrors. But you could equally argue that it is the recent Nazi horrors, the death camps, which account for Eliot's affront. In 1947, the accusation inevitably came charged with the penumbra of the Holocaust. I think the poetry can be defended, as I have in my study *T.S. Eliot* (2006).

However, in the deliberately unguarded letters to Emily Hale there are instances of anti-Semitism: he asks

for a 20 percent quota on Jews attending his classes at Harvard; he wonders, on the subject of a Jewish female mimic, 'why there is something diabolic about so many Jews?' The Tandy family, his friends, adopt a German Jewish child: Eliot says '*it* is not at all objectionably Jewish to look at' [my italics]. He says of Stephen Spender that he 'is all that I should dislike, being a half-Jew, an invert and a communist, but in whom I feel a curious physical attraction in spite of all that'. Late in life, he jokes with his cousin Eleanor Hinckley that photographs of him have 'a villainous squint or a Jewish physiognomy'. We have already encountered this earlier (26 September 1934): 'I am not surprised that you do not like the photograph of You [Emily Hale]. I admit that I would not show it to anyone who did not know you already –it is neither Jewish nor Vapid, and conveys a good deal to those who know you already – I should not exhibit to anyone who had never seen you – but I had an enlargement made for myself – but it does not look a fraction so Semitic as a picture which Ottoline [Morrell] took of me and sent to Hayward, and though[t] excellent, and which is really disgusting.' Elsewhere (16 August 1935) he repudiates 'filthy photographs of me', singling one out as 'less repulsive, because it looks less Jewish'.

In Volume 2, though, there are counter-indicators. Crawford reports that Eliot, once he had read the transcripts, deplored Pound's rantings on Rome radio: 'No one could read these outpourings and regard the writer as sane.' Yet he defended his friend even as he deprecated his politics in private: 'I do not see why I should continue to accept from you [Pound] insults to my nationality or to my religion. The latter includes the Jewish religion.' He was scathing about Mosley and the Blackshirts. He denounced the Nuremberg Laws against Jews in September 1941 in the *Christian News-Letter*. He wrote to Horace Kallen asking help for John Amon, a Viennese Jewish refugee. He assisted the German Jewish composer, Richard Fuchs, who had been in Dachau.

This letter to Emily Hale (29 March 1938) is typical: 'While I am distressed for the fate of the Jews in Vienna, I do hope that all the university professors will not come and settle here: there are enough Jews in the English universities as it is.' Sympathy and anti-Semitism in the same sentence, I would say. You might argue that Eliot feared anti-Semitism as a likely, even inevitable, consequence of large numbers of Jews. He often says that anti-Semitism isn't a problem in England, with the implication that it could be, given a large influx of Jews. Is that anti-Semitic or merely pragmatic? A question answered, you might think, by Eliot's assertion to Emily Hale (27 January 1939) that 'there is no denying that Jews in the mass are antipathetic'. I'm not so sure. The remark is preceded by this: 'I am concerned about the refugees – if they are allowed to collect indefinitely in Britain there is a great risk of eventual anti-Semitism here: but where are they to go?'

Anthony Julius would have us believe that Eliot concealed a virulent anti-Semitism. What kind of anti-Semite fears the rise of anti-Semitism?

You will recall that, in *After Strange Gods* (1933), Eliot infamously wrote that 'any large number of free-thinking

Jews [was] undesirable'. Crawford thinks this is a simple reflection of Eliot's anti-Semitic inheritance from his family. I wonder. Maybe the emphasis should be placed on *large number.* This was an age of immigration quotas. When Louis Menand wrote about Eliot and Anti-Semitism in the *New York Review of Books* (6 June 1996), Eliot's qualifications – 'free-thinking' and 'any large number' – both went missing. It became, in Menand's account, 'the direct reference to the undesirability of Jews'. There's a difference.

In December 1938, Sidney Dark, the editor of the *Church Times*, solicited Eliot's signature to a letter denouncing the rise of anti-Semitism in England. Eliot sympathised but withheld his signature. Crawford cites contemporary reports of German discrimination against the Jews – an implicit reproach to Eliot. But he also instances Eliot's personal assistance to individual Jews. Eliot argued that potential anti-Semites – 'bus conductors or small tobacconists or any of the unemployed or discontented' – were not readers of the *Church Times*, so the protest would be unprofitable – moral grandstanding, preaching to the converted.

Nor did Eliot sign a manifesto against anti-Semitism organised by Margaret Gardiner, the secretary of the Academic Freedom Committee, in July 1939. He believed that 'it is very easy to express sympathy with sufferers abroad, when what they want is practical help; and such statements may only exasperate the persecuted and irritate the persecutors.' He concluded: 'I believe that the important moment for collective statements about anti-semitism will be later, if, as is possible, that mania is further exploited in this country.' Eliot was always anxious that cynical politicians – 'the anti-Semitic Fascist political movement' – might use anti-Semitism as a lever to achieve political power.

Overall, I think there is a contradiction between Eliot's considered and unconsidered, off-the-cuff opinions. They co-existed. I don't mean to be provocative when I cite Primo Levi's sensible, hard-won, universal assertion: 'Occurrences like this astonish because they conflict with the image we have of man in harmony with himself, coherent, monolithic; and they should not astonish because that is not how man is. Compassion and brutality can coexist in the same individual and in the same moment, despite all logic; and for all that, compassion itself eludes logic.'

In 1951, at the ICA, in front of Eliot, Emanuel Litvinoff read out a poem, 'To T S Eliot', attacking him for his attitude to the Jews: 'Bleistein is my relation'. Stephen Spender, who was present, objected: 'I felt he was classing Mr Eliot with the people who committed atrocities in concentration camps.' Correct. Eliot isn't the equivalent of Franz Stangl. There is a moral asymmetry here, no moral equivalence. We should beware what Kundera calls moral exhibitionism. We should all calm down. It isn't a Cartesian clear and distinct perception. It isn't clear-cut and one-sided. I think Leonard Woolf was right to say Eliot was 'slightly anti-Semitic in the sort of way which is not uncommon' – and that he 'would have denied it quite genuinely'. As he did.

From *sky doc*

JOE CARRICK-VARTY

Once upon a time when suicide was getting everything I need

then I'm gone but it's not stealing

violence and all the self-harm that lilts

boys will be boys someone said

when we lined up on that hill

overlooking the city maybe

we had come to finish our fathers

maybe to finish ourselves

Once upon a time when suicide was say the magic word

and uncle Gary will appear I once

opened the door to my dad's middle brother

having not seen him in two years

he looked pink it was bonfire night

my dad hanging a Catherine wheel

recounted to a neighbour his brother

on our doorstep full up on class A

Once upon a time when suicide was not the least bit romantic

one Christmas my nana ran a bath

and never came back my dad had this plan

to visit Thailand something

about a turtle he had seen on TV

like wishing the film would end different

for the longest time I believed

he had gone to find the turtle

Once upon a time when suicide was walking the lip

      of the volcano they say insanity

      is doing the same thing over and over

      and expecting different results

      can this relate to patterns of thought

      if you think about dying enough

      but you wake up again you brush your teeth

      you put on your dad's favourite blue sweater

Once upon a time when suicide was an infinity pool

      with panoramic views and I wasn't brave enough

      to open my eyes underwater

      until the morning of checkout

      heading for a taxi fully clothed

      I took the plunge suicide with megaphone

      is holding a protest who knows if I saw

      what I needed to see in that water

Once upon a time when suicide was a cat called Minnie

      who could hardly lift her head to drink

      but on the day of her choosing

      climbed the shed then disappeared

      forever my dad long gone

      would have called her a dark horse

      in need of something to bury

      we planted a rose under the cherry tree

Three Poems

ALEXANDRA CORRIN-TACHIBANA

Unpacking our relationship

Love bombing

Yamashita Tatsuro's belting out ballads, on the ラジオ, as we set off for Nagano to ski. Your fingers tap tap on my knee. Then, you're serenading me, a Beach Boys cover: *Please Let Me Wonder*, about our future. Tell me to give back my ex his ring. Throw away my wedding album. Phone me in your lunch hour, to say you love *chubby girls*. Although you dated an air hostess with *great tits*. You hang a heart around my neck. But are not satisfied. It's smaller than displayed on the Internet.

Cigar incident

Remember the day you took me and my black eyes skiing? Lamie said, *things can't be that bad if you two managed to go skiing*. But he wasn't with you as we inched up the mountain. You pushed me to have a cigar the night before. Even though we quit. The cool guy and his wife with colleagues after Single Malts. And my black eyes? My fault. For not leaving you to sulk. For wanting to talk. But when you're out of sight, Lamie asks if I need to spend a few nights with him and his wife in California.

Mind games

Three times you pretend to throw your wedding ring away. I've fallen from esteemed *sensei* to distance learning student with no income. But you let me binge Desperate Housewives, drink Robert Mondavi wine, give me pocket money. And admit how well I click with Gloria & Lamie. It's easier when I'm at business dinners: you needn't speak a lot. And don't I scrub up well, in my black and white polka dots?

Birth Story

You abandon me at Kalamazoo hospital. Not able to perceive how alone I feel in a country where we are strangers. Not able to get that I'm not yet ready to choose a name. When Beatrice picks me up, makes me tea and drives me home, you say you were on the verge of calling the police. You dislike her immensely. Beatrice, who visits me when I give birth, brings homemade tacos to our house. She sees through you, to the real me.

Narcissistic personality disorder

Thirteen years later, in England, you're Chairman of the Japanese Golf Association. You buy prosecco, win tournaments. You write 特別な reports. Your face is on the web. Use Re-up hair tonic for men. Straighten your teeth. Everyone says you don't look in your fifties. And what of my modest poetry prize? You tell our son I can donate it to our domestic account. You can pay in less this month.

Gaslighting

When I'm marking homework, you say it's not appropriate to be working on a Saturday. Although you write *daily reports*, play Boxing Day golf. You ask if I've had a diagnosis of anxiety. Or if it's something hormonal. You should call my boss if he's *overloading me*. But you don't know his name. On a whim, you take my computer away. I have twenty minutes to remove my work files. Later, you say you were cleaning it up. It takes a professional to tell me, that this is not acceptable.

Snapshots from Beck Hide

On the lake born of mining activities, two swans, with grimy plumage. I ping you the photo. Tell you how they fought another pair for their stretch, the losers put to flight. Do you remember the mute swans at Windsor? Over 300 of them. Using the huge body of water as a runway for taking off. How ugly they were! I told you I preferred to see two, at a distance, their heads in a heart.

Mum warned me to stay away from swans. Just like she said never let the sun go down on an argument. A swan can break your leg if it believes that it's defending its territory. And although it might be an old wives' tale, I look past them, to a heron on a post, who's ignoring bold young geese congregating in the duckweed. Canada geese, an invasive species, you tell me: locusts of fresh water.

Later, I see flocks of blue-violet foxgloves, thriving in the clearing. Foxgloves, like giant Rocket Lollies: your favourite flower. They yield digoxin medicine, that tames your daughter's fluttering heartbeat. And although things are tricky between her and me right now, when I consider my own teenage son, I understand how grateful you are for this miracle flower.

And when I discover an old post on Instagram, of matchstick figures holding hands wrapped in a bubble labelled 'family', I get her struggle with me – an invader of her home. Feisty as a mute swan, she's preserving her patch. Noisily flapping and hissing, she's capable of hurtful blows. But, ultimately, it's bluster and show. She does not do serious damage.

Julie Andrews' Honesty

Neither of us is an oil painting, it's true. But
especially true on WhatsApp. With my huge
Italian glasses on, I look like Maureen Lipman
in the British Telecom adverts.
I am not, you say, the woman you met
in person coming smiling down the platform,
in my sunflower dress. But at least
I'm more attractive in the flesh.
Onscreen, you're dripping like a Walls ice-cream,
and what with all my wondering what Mum
might make of a *silver-splitter*,
sometimes, I question why we bother. Except
for how hard you make me laugh. When I say
your bum is pert and mine is ample, and you say:
Pert & Ample, like a firm of solicitors.
Or when you dance around your office,
doing the curious moves that only you can do.
And then there's talk of *butlering*
in the noddy, of waking up to
alfresco morning breasts.
And I love the way you notice how I move my head
to emphasize a point, as *only a teacher* can do.
Do it again, you say. And then there's
my *fucking Julie Andrews' Honesty*,
which you've come to love.

Louis MacNeice's Hat

HUGH THOMSON

Louis MacNeice was interested in clothes. Geoffrey Grigson describes him as 'well-dressed', as does his friend John Hilton, who adds in a note to *The Strings Are False*, MacNeice's uncompleted autobiography, that even as a student at Oxford, Louis tried to dress elegantly.

There are several allusions in the poetry to the difference between a made-to-measure and an off-the-peg suit. When MacNeice meets Yeats for the first time in 1934, he is impressed by the older poet's 'smooth light suit and just sufficiently crooked bowtie'. The alluring Muse he mentions in 'Autumn Journal' wears not just stockings and suspenders, but is 'dressed by Schiaparelli, with a pill-box hat'.

Many photographs show MacNeice in a brown trilby – a hat designed so that one can tilt it slightly askew; so that one can look at the world askance. It is the hat of a man who likes going to the races or rugby matches, or who stands in a pub leaning against the pillar. In a contact sheet of publicity photos for Faber, MacNeice is bare-headed for the first dozen or so and then starts wearing his hat, almost as if he felt naked without it. Certainly he looks better with it.

Critics like Ian Hamilton have talked of MacNeice's 'aloofness', although there are times as well when he can be very direct. When he rams the hat more horizontally over his head. And he undoubtedly does so in 'Autumn Journal'.

How has 'Autumn Journal' worn? Since MacNeice's long narrative poem was published in 1939, its reputation has grown steadily over the years, along with MacNeice's own, helped by promoters such as Paul Muldoon and Glyn Maxwell. The loose-leaf format of a journal, with its ability to mix the diurnal with the casual, the political and the romantic, plays to all his strengths.

As the poem opens, he is writing the journal as his train travels from Hampshire to London, in between looking out of the window. And that shock of moving from the country suburbs to the city – from clipped yew hedges and tennis courts to the crowd emerging from Piccadilly Circus tube – from Persephone's journey into hell to her return in the spring – is the springboard which gives the poem its energy and sustains its thousands of lines:

> And so to London and down the ever-moving Stairs
> Where a warm wind blows the bodies of men together
> And blows apart their complexes and cares. (Canto i)

Part of the success and charm of 'Autumn Journal' comes from the use of what MacNeice described to T.S. Eliot as 'an elastic quatrain': two of the four lines rhyme, but the others have soft feminine endings which don't:

> Spider, spider twisting tight –
> But the watch is wary beneath the pillow –
> I am afraid on the web of night
> When the window is fingered by the shadows
> of branches... (ii)

The effect is for the verse to flow from the contraction of each rhymed line to the expansion of the intervening unrhymed one, which enables him to vary the pace – essential over such a long, book-length poem – but also suits his poetic character. The lines alternately engage and disengage.

MacNeice's friends commented how he could be in congenial surroundings but not necessarily genial; that he was a detached observer. As Ian Hamilton noted after his death: 'Those who had social dealings with MacNeice tended to scratch their heads and remember nothing very much. They spoke of him as a "dark horse" and recalled his lack of warmth, his silences, his impenetrable moods. He was forever in the pub, they'd say, but not really *of* the pub. He kept himself not just to himself for himself. For, that's to say, the poems.'

In an essay called 'Modern Poetry', written in 1937 just before 'Autumn Journal', MacNeice declared, in a well-known call to arms: 'I would have a poet able bodied, fond of talking, a reader of the newspapers, capable of pity and laughter, informed in economics, appreciative of women, involved in personal relationships, actively interested in politics, susceptible to physical impressions.'

This is perhaps more aspirational than a straight-faced description of himself. On the basis of quotes like these, MacNeice has been sometimes labelled a 'worldly poet', with what is perhaps his most famous poem, 'Snow', held up in evidence:

> World is suddener than we fancy it.

World is crazier and more of it than we think,
Incorrigibly plural.

But care is needed. For a poet to be worldly is almost a contradiction in terms – otherwise they'd be out making money and a living, not sitting in a quiet corner writing poetry, surely the least worldly of occupations. And certainly the least profitable.

Many writers would like to be worldly; some have become adept at painting themselves as such. But even Byron, Rochester, Hemingway and the most out there of 'worldly' literary personas had a quieter, more reflective side which they couldn't help revealing. Much of their literary energy comes from wanting to appear more worldly and engaged than they actually were; the writing became a sublimation of that wish for engagement.

MacNeice has to remind himself that the world might be both sudden and crazier than he had thought – 'more of it than we think'. He doesn't know it. His face is pressed to the window pane, looking out at the snow. He is a classicist who in 'Autumn Journal' is intrigued, entranced but often confused by the modern world around him. A classicist who knows, as shown by his friend and mentor E.R. Dodds in *The Greeks and the Irrational,* that the calm classical world we think of as a 'model of logic and lucidity' is fringed by the wilder world around it: 'the bloody Bacchanals on the Thracian hills', as MacNeice describes the contrast in Canto ix.

In 'Autumn Journal' (which uses the word 'world' no less than twenty-six times), he fantasises about what 'a future of action' would be like:

Where I shall play the gangster or the sheikh,
Kill for the love of killing, make the world my sofa,
Unzip the women and insult the meek. (iii)

At the same time he recognises that his more reflective nature means that he has to force himself to 'look up and outwards'.

MacNeice's previous books had been collections of more conventional-length poems, noticeable for their abrupt changes of tone and personality as he played out the different aspects – or roles – of the ideal 'able bodied poet' he had prescribed in 'Modern Poetry'. In the longer loose-leaf format of 'Autumn Journal', he was able to combine and contrast all of them in the same work. It was the first full-length narrative poem of his own he published, although he had translated Greek plays like Aeschylus's *Agamemnon* and experimented on verse letters with Auden in their joint and playful *Letters from Iceland*.

To describe 'Autumn Journal' as 'autobiographical' or lyric is to miss the point. This is not 'The Prelude', in which Wordsworth builds a composite picture of the organic growth of a poet. Instead it shows how disparate are his daily impressions and impulses, made more acute in 1938, when the poem is set, by the febrile sense that we are on the eve of a war.

... Hitler yells on the wireless,
    The night is damp and still
And I hear dull blows on wood outside my window;

They are cutting down the trees on Primrose
    Hill.
The wood is white like the roast flesh of chicken,
    Each tree falling like a closing fan;
No more looking at the view from seats beneath the
    branches,
    Everything is going to plan. (vii)

MacNeice himself addressed the issue of the poet's narrative voice and whether it was lyric – a term he thought 'a terrible red herring', as it implied a spontaneous outpouring of emotion – or whether it was better thought of as *'dramatic'* [his italics], the poet positioning himself on various different parts of the stage for 'a monodrama' ('Experiences with Images', 1949).

Edna Longley speculated that 'the English suspicion of MacNeice often derives from a puritanical objection to dramatic stylization, to the poet "hiding" behind a façade'. She draws attention to the way he preferred, in his own words, 'a controlled flamboyance of diction' to Wordsworth's plain speaking 'crusade of homespun'.

Although they are rarely spoken of in the same breath, 'Autumn Journal' has more in common with 'The Waste Land' and that poem's original working title, 'Doing the Police in Different Voices'. It is likewise a young man's poem – MacNeice was thirty-two – and at times allows the rhythms of a city to propel it.

In a letter to T.S. Eliot when Faber were due to publish 'Autumn Journal', MacNeice described the work as 'not strictly a journal but giving the tenor of my emotional experiences during that period. It is about everything which from first-hand experience I consider important.'
'First-hand' was crucial – as Eliot noted in his reply:

I have read through the 'Autumn Journal', and I think it is very good indeed. At times I was much moved, and what is still more unusual in the case of a single long poem, I found that I read it through without my interest flagging at any point. That is due partly to the dexterity with which you vary the versification, and, I think, to the fact that the imagery is all imagery of things lived through, and not merely chosen for poetic effectiveness. (7 February 1939)

One of the attractions of the poem is its surprising range: what's happening in politics, in love, in thought and in landscape – what one sees out of the window, as well as in the mirror. It is incorrigibly plural.

You whom I remember glad or tired,
Smiling in drink or scintillating anger,
Inopportunely desired
On boats, on trains, on roads when walking. (iv)

The end of his affair with the married Nancy Coldstream (who is not named) lies at the heart of the poem. It is dedicated more to her absence than presence.

And my common sense denies she is returning
And says, if she does return, she will not stay;
And my pride, in the name of reason, tells me to cut
    my losses

And call it a day.
Which, if I had the cowardice of my convictions,
  I certainly should do
But doubt still finds a loophole
  To gamble on another rendezvous. [xi]

There is an honesty about his mixed emotions. Mac-
Neice does not put Coldstream on a pedestal.

...at times malicious
  And generous at times.
Whose kaleidoscopic ways are all authentic,
  Whose truth is not of a statement but of a dance
So that even when you deceive your deceits are merely
  Technical and of no significance. [xi]

The wonderful soft and false rhyme of dance / signifi-
cance, with the sudden hardening needed to complete
the step, are typical of the adroit choreography. If just
the sections dealing with the affair were extracted from
'Autumn Journal', they would form one of the most
intriguing and thoughtful love poems of the century –
and one which manages to remain remarkably
clear-sighted about both his own shortcomings and
those of his lover.

In a letter to E.R. Dodds, he says that he 'nearly had a
breakdown' over the relationship and its failure, and
later, to a subsequent lover, Eleanor Clark, that he 'wrote
a lot of it ['Autumn Journal'] when in a very bad way over
my old friend [Nancy]'. Being emotionally punch-drunk
intensified his perceptions both of the world and of him-
self; MacNeice was always interested in exploring con-
tradictory sides of his own personality.

Just a few years later, he wrote 'Corner Seat', a short
poem about his reflection in the train window as he
travels:

Suspended in a moving night
The face in the reflected train
Looks at first sight as self-assured
As your own face – But look again:

Windows between you and the world
Keep out the cold, keep out the fright;
Then why does your reflection seem
So lonely in the moving night?

MacNeice is self-conscious, in the best sense. He ques-
tions his own assumptions. What other poet of the 1930s
would have pointed out that while, yes, he wanted the
proletariat to be enfranchised, he was aware of his own
privileges?

And now the tempter whispers 'But you also
  Have the slave-owner's mind,
Would like to sleep on a mattress of easy profits,
  To snap your fingers or a whip and find
Servants or houris ready to wince and flatter
  And build with their degradation your self-esteem;
What you want is not a world of the free in function
  But a niche at the top, the skimmings of the cream.'
(iii)

In recent years MacNeice has been reclaimed as an
Irish poet by Seamus Heaney, Derek Mahon and their
contemporaries, and disengaged from the tandem bike
he once rode with Auden. Paul Muldoon's *Faber Book of
Contemporary Irish Poetry* of 1986 gave MacNeice a prom-
inent place. There are elements of Yeats – about whom
MacNeice wrote a book just after 'Autumn Journal' – in
the similar dramatic personae that MacNeice at times
adopts: the disappointed lover; the engaged political
observer; the poet in his tower grappling with metaphys-
ical complexities or with classical antiquity. And the
Irish voice lends itself to the mixture of hard and soft
that MacNeice likes so much and that one can hear in
recordings of him reading his verse, where a little bit of
hard Ulster still underlies the soft anglicised accent. G.S.
Fraser, who attended one of the last of such readings,
described how 'his fine poet's voice, with its aspirated
dentals, its noise of determined snorting through a per-
manent mild nasal catarrh, was an Irish countryman's,
almost an Irish peasant's, voice'.

Perhaps when one sees MacNeice with his tilted hat,
one should think not of the disengaged Englishman
being reticent, but of a more sardonic Irishman consid-
ering whether to make an astute remark, or who could
buy the next drink. And of whether he should start per-
forming, and with which voice. And that he would only
say something if he really had something to say. Which
he did. A hat, like one of the cigarettes he constantly
smoked, is a good prop to have on stage.

Four Poems

ANTONY HUEN

Chinatown, London

after Allen Ginsberg

When I go to Chinatown, I get matcha ice cream and never get mistaken.
The motherly owner speaks my mother tongue with an accent.
All-you-can-eat places serve frozen spring rolls, and I
pay for overpriced egg waffles. They come with sprinkles.
No pudding in the shape of koi, in a pool of condensed milk.

On the train to York I give the table a wipe, opening
the ice-cold sushi box and the wasabi sachet,
made in China. I break the chopsticks apart to pick up
a mouthful of jasmine rice mixed with salmon flakes.
I taste the sashimi and pickled ginger from home.

That Day

Tricked by my bestie, I landed in Berlin.
She didn't and I shared a room
with a man with big feet. He snored.

In the morning we checked in together.
What I never came close to: a coat of my height,
the coffee-smelling hello, ramen-curls.

He posed before the giant Lego giraffe,
playing Leonid, then Erich in the murals.
In dad's coat, I could barely turn my head.

We walked into a concert hall for the loo.
The sky turned black as we left
for the island of museums,

managing a touch of the marbles.
He grabbed my forearm lest I fall
on the ice. The day ended with mulled wine.

The next day I got lost, leaving a yellow palace.
My first hitch-hike, a pierced tongue.
I tucked in my shirt. He repeated *xie-xie*.

That Night

In a wool overcoat, you walked me to the house
through the brick arch, where ivy leaves hung
like the tartan scarf around your neck.

Like my childhood one – two-storey,
with a chimney and eight windows
in the shape of our word for *paddy*.

On the sofa, Japanese snacks, yoga mats,
Tesco bags and Argos rice cookers.
On the table, mayo stains and opened sachets.

In a sticky cabinet, your crockery still
in bubble wrap. The stairs were squeaky
and your Levi's were low-rise.

Your room door opened to the scent
of incense and Tenenbaums décor.
Through the steamed-up window, a fence

and a sycamore tree. The tour ended
with hot ginseng tea, a Cantopop singalong
and my *no* to your M&S cotton towel.

Ekphrasis

Type in your name and
the two armours carved into
the Sheldonian Theatre
dissolve into a milestone in my life –
my leaning on an inscribed stone slab.
*If you fail to reach the Great Wall, you
aren't a true man.* But the truth is
we dream of riding flying elephants
and galloping horses, seeing ourselves in
the mirrors – a dream that keeps returning
like flies hovering at night before
landing on the lit laptop screen.

Three Poems

JULITH JEDAMUS

Encounter

Late November. Heading toward Morden
on the Northern Line, I looked up from my phone
as the doors closed, provoked not by a voice
or a brush with a masked man but by a delicious
smell that floated in at Chalk Farm
though no one had got on – the smell of resinous
pines, orange blossom and pelargonium.
No one else seemed to notice.

What invisible thing carried it in?
The Northern Line's not known for its perfume.
Something brushed my cheek, spoke
inaudibly. No one gave us a second look.
Then it came to me: had I, near-ghost,
been found by another ghost?

'Adam and Eve'
(Lucas Cranach, 1526)

Notice Eve's pale skin, Adam's perplexed expression.
Then lower your gaze to the right-hand corner,
where a young roebuck sips his own reflection.

Admire his naive horns and immaculate hide, not yet
bloodied by ruts or rough sex. Is he prone
to the same weakness as Narcissus? Not yet...

He can't be accused of vanity until Adam
bites the apple and sin rushes in.
Roebuck, boar, lion, heron: all seem

glossy and clean, like the apples that hang
from these still boughs. Nor do angels
– never Luther's friends – hang

in this dawn sky, pitying the roebuck, who's poised
on the verge of violent knowledge. Hunters and fear
pursue him, once the apple's twice tasted.

The Gardener

She was a daisy, chaste
and plain. Her Master the sun

turned her face; her brother
the deceiver was a trillium

basking on the floor of Amherst
birch-glades. Chrysanthemums

smelled like her sister Vinnie.
Mabel the adulteress crowded

her days like peonies: frilled,
showy, hard to please.

No wonder she longed for frost,
the blonde assassin, to leave

her alone, free to mine
winter's quarries and trim

sapphires to tidy facets.
Wary of noon, white as jessamine,

she walked at twilight picking bedstraw,
robin-run-away, Sol's seal, bastard

pennyroyal, fringed gentians.
Shy and Puritan, purple as Tyre

or Cleopatra's gown, gentians were
for her the most New England-y of flowers –

and so is she, suave paradox who sows
gamboge seeds in the mind's furrows.

An Intonation of Place

A Poetic Journey with John McGahern and Alistair MacLeod

ÁGNES CSERHÁTI

At the Belfast Festival in 1968, John McGahern began his lecture, 'I am only interested in poetry, which occurs more often in verse than in prose'. Among the audience were Tyrone Guthrie, Sean O'Riada, John Montague and Seamus Heaney. McGahern had published *The Dark* three years before to uproar and censorship. He was cast out from his teaching job. He left Ireland. He went back. Was he openly declaring himself a poet? And among such eminent compatriots?

To answer this question, I can only go a circuitous route and as far back as 2000, when as a postgraduate based in London, I travelled all over. In October, it was a four-day trek in Pembrokeshire. Hiking boots, a backpack with a change of clothes, and two cameras (one with colour film, the other with black and white), were all that I carried with me. There was hardly anyone along the coast path, and with every image captured through my lens, a burgeoning sense of self emerged. It was invigorating. Yet elusive. There was something *other* apparent as I stood beside Carreg Samson, my hand warmed by the capstone, or at Whitesands Bay, watching a track of woad get pushed along the shoreline. Unmistakeably, this was bard country. But what did that mean?

It happened, too, later that winter, alone at the Rocks of Solitude as I touched the cold, wet wall of rock and traced my fingers along the gryke, then made my way back over Gannochy Bridge with the intrepid River Esk surging below, and through a forest of birch and pines where the Highlands and Lowlands meet. It was Christmas, yet this place was much older than God. A place of return, though I had only just arrived. An intonation of place. A voice that was *other*, but held close.

I had only encountered such a sense of place in my reading of Alistair MacLeod, which I brought with me to London. His short stories were a single elegy for Cape Breton, Nova Scotia, and I carried with me the weight of a son's love for his father, who 'had never been intended for a fisherman [and] had always wanted to go to the university', and who gave his life so his son could choose for himself. Though Heaney's 'The Grauballe Man', with his 'chin... a visor / raised above the vent / of his slashed throat // that has tanned and toughened. / The cured wound / open[ing] inwards to a dark / elderberry place', speaks as clearly, the final image in 'The Boat' is as harrowing in its detail and realism as anything I've read before or since:

His hands were shredded ribbons, as were his feet which had lost their boots to the suction of the sea, and his shoulders came apart in our hands when we tried to move him from the rocks. And the fish had eaten his testicles and the gulls had pecked out his eyes and the white-green stubble of his whiskers had

continued to grow in death, like the grass on graves, upon the purple, bloated mass that was his face. There was not much left of my father, physically, as he lay there with the brass chains on his wrists and the seaweed in his hair.

In an interview given in 2005, MacLeod invokes Coleridge's axiom of poetry, to which he adds, 'I think prose should also aspire to use the best language'. Certainly, MacLeod is one to use 'the best words in their best order'; so then, is he pushing the prose envelope to the brink of poetry and thereby declaring himself a poet, too? Well, I doubt he would have put it that way, but by McGahern's standards, my own view is that MacLeod is equally a poet who happens to write in prose. Yes, there is the precision, but also, as McGahern himself once said of MacLeod, a 'careful work [that] never appears to stray outside what quickens it... a largeness, of feeling, of intellect, of vision'. A voice that is *other* but held close.

This became clear in my introduction to McGahern's work a few years after my time in London. By then, I had gone to Sligo (to hear Heaney read at the Hawk's Well Theatre), and that mystical sense of *other* was there again as I stood atop Knocknarea, beside the cairn, looking onto Strandhill and the sea below. This, too, was bard country, like that of Carreg Samson and the Rocks of Solitude. It was also McGahern country.

It was here that McGahern spent two weeks each summer as a child after his mother died and he lived with his father and sisters in the barracks at Roscommon, and to which he returns repeatedly in his short stories and novels. I held no camera in hand, as what I might have seen through the lens had already been captured in McGahern's words that echoed in the immediacy of how the 'wind, blowing the length of the level strand, tugged at their hair and clothes'. McGahern continues in *Amongst Women*:

This time when he reached for her she came into his arms. Her hair and face tasted of sea spray.... In a hollow between high dunes they spread out raincoats on the sand and kicked away their shoes. She then, half-kneeling, pulled away her underthings and moved close to him for warmth. He put down his clothes over his thighs and entered her... Above them the wind whipped only at the highest tussocks and the ocean sounded far away.

Besides the alliterative 'l' in 'length' and 'level', the 's' in 'sea spray', the 'h' in 'hollow' and 'high', and the 'w' in 'wind whipped' that makes certain of a deliberateness of words placed 'in their best order', it is the image of lovers caught in their need within the isolation of a relenting landscape – the hollow protects them from wind and sea and sight – that arrests our senses and imprints itself upon the mind.

Image is of paramount importance to McGahern. Taking his cue from Proust, for McGahern, the image relates cyclically to vision and rhythm: 'The vision, that still and private world which each of us possesses and which others cannot see, is brought to life in rhythm – rhythm being little more than the instinctive movements of the vision as it comes to life and begins its search for the image.' There is also something integral and ontological at work, a 'straining towards the one image that will never come, the image on which our whole life took its most complete expression once, that would completely express it again in this bewilderment between our beginning and our end.'

Rhythm is perhaps easiest to pin down – for McGahern, it 'encompasses not only the rhythm of the sounds in the sentences, but also includes repetitions of images, words and phrases within the work, which he has compared to refrains in verse' (Stanley van der Ziel). Among a plethora of examples of such refrain in McGahern are the figures of Barnaby and Bartleby in Abbey Street as well as the narrator's 'empty hands' and 'uproarious mirth' in 'Doorways'; or the white face and the blue steel hands of the watch in 'Gold Watch'; and very clearly in 'The rain anywhere is bad, but at the sea, at the sea, it's the end', and 'the rain, the rain at the sea, is deadly' in 'Strandhill, the Sea'. Van der Ziel observes in MacLeod's writing a style that 'is very close to that of McGahern in the preciseness of its expression and the fineness of its idiosyncratic rhythms'. A handful of examples from MacLeod includes the repetition of place names and spoken words in Gaelic, such as '*Àite na cruinneachadh*', 'the meeting place' in 'Island'; or the answer, '*Se mi-fhìn*', 'It's myself' to the urgency of '*Cò a th'ann?*', 'Who's there? Who's there?' in 'Vision'; Archibald's noncommittal 'Mmmm' in 'The Tuning of Perfection'; and particularly the phrase '*ille bhig ruiadh*', 'the little red-haired boy' amidst the several manifestations of the name Alexander MacDonald, and Calum's Celtic ring in *No Great Mischief*. A developing mnemonics of sound, sense and image is prevalent. This much is clear.

Less clear is how 'the image that will never come' can establish itself in poetry at all. Here I will turn to Patrick Friesen who posits that 'one function of poetry is to be a song of longing for what is not there, nor ever was'. He continues, 'Not longing for the memory itself, but for something outside of memory, the absence which is the context of memory; the state of longing in and of itself.' The bewilderment, then, of which McGahern speaks, might be a longing for an image that eludes expression, but that still makes its presence felt in its very absence. In this, the act of image-seeking is poetry itself, while that sense of *other*, that longing 'for something outside of memory' that can be felt in places that seem to defy a passage of time, is what I mean by bard country. Whether it's a Neolithic dolmen or a mythical cairn by the seaside, or a rock formation billions of years old set in the riverbank, they sing of absence, something that will never be captured by a camera lens. McGahern, however, as poet and pilgrim of bard country, is able to mould these sensibilities into something coherent and immediate for all that they hinge on absence, that in a moment of revelation for the narrator in 'Doorways', at least, brings the dead and the oblivious together, where 'all seemed… equally awash in time and indistinguishable, the same mute human presence beneath the unchanging sky'. In longing, '[w]e were all waiting in the doorways'.

One thing about bard country that needs saying, though it is obvious, is that it centres on place and a return to place. Part of the process of searching for the lost image is a return to place, 'the constant reference point' from which 'memories associated with it transform it into an anchor of the self itself' (Dennis Sampson). McGahern's Strandhill and the sea are such reference points throughout his oeuvre, pinning characters against a landscape and in so doing revealing their innermost selves. Michael's repeated escapes to Strandhill in *Amongst Women* are a sexual awakening, though in his bewilderment is also something he 'couldn't comprehend'.

Let us also not forget the longing implicit in the return to place, especially if that place somehow changes. In 'Gold Watch', the narrator looks forward to gathering the hay in his annual retreat to his father's farm but is at last confronted by change that becomes a kind of displacement he can't fathom:

Though I had come intending to make it my last summer at the hay, I now felt a keen outrage that it had been ended without me…. A bird moved in some high branch, but afterwards the silence was so deep it began to hurt, and the longing grew for the bird or anything to stir again.

Bard country exists between the silences where the straining for the lost image becomes that elusive sense of *other*, a voice that sings despite its tacit absence.

MacLeod's avowal of such a state is his use of elegy in his own oeuvre, a poetic form that is a lament for loss. In his case, he laments the loss for a way of life in Cape Breton, mainly of the fishermen, miners, loggers, and the stalwart women who set their lives alongside theirs. Cape Breton is the constant reference point to which MacLeod's characters return. In *No Great Mischief*, Calum's final return is also a final farewell: 'This is the man who carried me on his shoulders when I was three. Carried me across the ice from the island, but could never carry me back again.' Place becomes displacement; Cape Breton becomes the absence of place and the lives once lived there – spent mackerel thrown back into the sea.

The ontological implication can perhaps be better conceived in the concept of *hiraeth*, a Welsh word for which there is no direct English translation, but which may be understood as 'homesickness, longing, nostalgia, and yearning, for a home that you cannot return to, no longer exists, or maybe never was'. This recalls Friesen's belief in poetry being a means of longing 'for something outside of memory' and McGahern's 'bewilderment between our beginning and our end' in his search for the lost image.

In Heaney's words, moreover, in relation to what is perceived – let's say the murmur of the sea at Whitesands Bay or at Strandhill – and the poet's role in making it come to life, 'it is essential that the vision of reality which poetry offers should be transformative'. The realistic descriptions of the mutilated bodies in 'The Grauballe Man' and in 'The Boat', for example, are there to speak out of the void of death on the victims' behalf, and to invite the listener to a place *in extremis*, where he can 'make his soul [and] bring himself to wholeness' (Heaney). In other words, it is not enough to simply strain after the lost image, but to experience mystery in the straining and in the confrontation with the limitations of human existence itself.

And so the camera hangs idly by my side as I fall to silence in the landscapes of longing and realise my own becoming. Our return to such a point *is* bard country, that sense of *other*, a presence in absence, a voice held close. To have arrived in bard country, as well, through the voices of McGahern and MacLeod – through their particular visions, refrains, image-seeking, and sea change to our souls – suggests of something more than stories told in prose (however strong such prose may be). Suggests, in fact, that both McGahern and MacLeod are decidedly poets, albeit in prose.

Six Poems

REBECCA WATTS

Personal Effects

My mother keeps parts of me under her bed.
Parts she gave; parts
she took back.

Folded into tissues
and tucked inside envelopes
like little wage packets

are twists of my hair, my teeth,
my bracelet from the hospital –
things I never asked for,

whose capture
I didn't resist, and above which,
dark nights, she tosses and turns.

I don't miss them,
since they have been replaced
with new hair, new teeth,

and I could buy myself a bracelet
any time. But when I see her sometimes
seeing me

smiling for a photo
or tightening my ponytail
or taking off my watch and placing it on the windowsill

I wonder if she's considering
claiming other relics
that one day could remind us both who we are.

Autobiographia Literaria

Teachers
I adored who
would not love me! Misses
Warwick and Charlesworth – young, pretty
women

made of
curls and white musk –
how I cried, wanting to
be like them! and how my crying
made them

hate me!
so instead of
understanding they showed
me to the reading corner, where
cross-legged

I sat
facing the wall
of books, blocking the screams
from the playground, teaching myself
to lose

myself
in the other
worlds, which some faraway
kind person wanted me to know
are there

The Landscapes of My Childhood

The landscapes of my childhood were cosy:
stopped-clock church towers nestled among oak and ash,
a static river mirroring a static sky.

I am still among the landscapes of my childhood.
When I walk out in the mornings, hardly a thing moves:
a squirrel, a magpie, a few pigeons mostly.

I'd like to arrive in the landscapes of my adulthood –
to feel precarious, scared even, at where I've come to,
its heights and precipices and many shadowed crevices.

Large mammals likely thrive in the landscapes of my adulthood –
gorillas and elephants and giraffes, all wholly
real, not merely actors in a showcase for a zoo,

and each day is as striking as a zebra there, and as clear,
and the flora abounds, very hungry, and grows huge.
In the landscapes of my adulthood I think I'll meet you,

who'll tell me things I don't already know, and be reassured
by my memories of the landscapes of my childhood
as we hunker and sing shanties in our cabin in the storm.

I am still among the landscapes of my childhood.

I Want To Be the Orange

I want to be the orange.
The blueberry has merits –
special powers relative
to its size (a *superfruit*!)
– but is too easily lost,
tiny, accidentally
squashable, dusty, inter
rupted by its husky stalk,
soft, hard, sharp, sour, out-of-time.

I want to be the orange.
I want to be generous
and tough, vibrant and yielding,
delighted and protected,
largely idle, throwable
and catchable, and beaming
all the while – able to spare
my golden afterglow, so
sure am I that I was there.

There are some things your parents can't teach you;

they grip too tight. So it's a woman from
the other end of the village (Sonia,
apparently) who's jogging along
behind the purple bike with the fat white
tyres on the field next to the school this
sunny Saturday – her palm steadying
the back of the saddle, her fingers curled
beneath – panting encouraging words

to the small, shy girl in the red tracksuit
who grips the handlebars like a pilot
pushing off from tarmac, legs spinning like
propellers, her gaze so completely fixed
on what's ahead that she doesn't sense
the stranger's hand has already let go.

PRIVATE NO ACCESS

The animal in me is padding through woods in the rain,
        poking her nose in rabbit holes,
forging a channel through the bluebell sea
        which quivers in her wake.

The animal in me is rooting out spiders and insects,
        scuffing rich dirt beneath a dripping oak,
close and low-down tracking the scent of musk
        which spells out the name of her kind.

The birches' eyes are on her and she does not care,
        for she has the world on her side, the green
harkening follow-me world
        where every thing alive is permitted

and everything is alive. Her ears prick – momentary –
        at the crunch of gravel as someone about-heels
in deference to the sign. She runs
        and every wild-garlic star bursts open.

'Grace and Danger'

Fanny Howe and the rootedness of absence

IAN POPLE

Fanny Howe is a prolific and successful writer. Her prose has included fiction and non-fiction, the former short-listed for the Man Booker International. Her poetry has twice been short-listed for the Griffin Prize and she was a Griffin Prize judge in 2015. To date, she has published sixteen volumes of poetry, fifteen books of fiction and three volumes of non-fiction. In the UK, Howe has been published by presses usually associated with the British Poetry Revival. In 1995, Ken Edwards' Reality Street Editions published the poem sequence *O'Clock.* And in 1999, Paul Green's Spectacular Diseases published a *festschrift* entitled *A Folio for Fanny Howe.* This contained the sequence 'Q', as well as essays on her work from Rae Armantrout and Romana Huk, amongst others. The American L=A=N=G=U=A=G=E poet Michael Palmer published Howe's important essay 'The Contemporary Logos'. However, while Howe has some sympathy with a sense of language as 'alien: separate, other, outside', she has commented that this may yield only to 'words speaking to words'. In addition, the small body of criticism on her work tends to concentrate on the Christian commitments and substance shown in her poetry. In particular, these commentators have noted Howe's absorption of the work of twentieth-century Christian mystics such as Simone Weil and St Edith Stein. These are mystics who, Grace Jantzen comments, 'come across as skilled in linguistic usage, and not in one genre only but in many'. Don Cupitt, in turn, suggests that they are 'people highly conscious of language, people who convey their message, not by pointing to something outside language, but by the way they play games *with* language, tormenting it because it torments them, keeping to the rules in such a *wicked* way as to get round the rules'.

Albert Gelpi regards Emily Dickinson as a formative influence on the work of both Fanny and her sister Susan Howe's poetry. For Gelpi, Susan Howe's work has a 'sense of kinship with Dickinson in fracturing form as an act of dissent'. Susan Howe approaches Dickinson through the lens of history, in a diachronic way which feeds into L=A=N=G=U=A=G=E poetry. Gelpi sees the Dickinson influence on Fanny Howe, on the other hand, as extending to both technique and content. 'Her characteristically short, taut, sometimes witty poems are, like Dickinson's, dense and centripetal, inscribing moments of a spiritual and psychological quest, word by packed word, image by edged image'.

That spiritual quest offers what Howe, after Simone Weil, calls, in 'The Contemporary Logos', being 'rooted in the absence'. Howe quotes Weil, 'We must take the feeling of being at home into exile. We must be rooted in the absence of a place'. Being rooted in absence applies not only to place. This is also an absence of a particularised spiritual home as well, even where that absence seems located Catholicism. One consequence of this rootedness in absence is Howe's obsessive need to tussle with the transcendent; a spiritual home which language can only glancingly evoke.

Howe's *Selected Poems* (2000) starts with a poem sequence entitled 'Introduction to the World'. There is a world, certainly, but it is a world which *needs* an introduction because it is contingent, 'separate, other, outside'. This is a world where the process of that introduction can work both ways. Are we meeting that world for the first time, or is the poet introducing us to the poet's own, particular world? When 'Introduction to the World' was first published in a book of the same name, in 1986, it was prefaced with the comments,

I was taking a course called introduction to Spirituality, which concentrated on that mystical manifesto, The Gospel of John.

The taking of language from the outside was a part of the general loss of myself to a new awareness, which I consider a grace and a dangerous situation. The poems then became attempts at describing those qualities, which are indestructible.

Howe's sense of 'the general loss of myself to a new awareness' is based on her study of the Gospel of John with its resounding start, 'In the beginning was the Word and the Word was with God, and the Word was God. He was with God in the beginning.' The poem sequence 'Introduction to the World' might be titled 'Introduction to the Wor[l]d'. The Word offers a new awareness, which is not defined or made explicit, but it has two indestructible qualities – grace and danger. Such qualities might characterise the loss of self which the language precipitates. There is the danger in the loss of self, but the grace the Gospel offers is for a another, different self. The absent and present self incarnates, in Howe's phrase, 'a new awareness.' With that awareness, a new searching occurs, as shown in the final poem from that sequence:

I'll pay and bow out
For not hardship but the judiciary
Connected the test of time
To penalty
I in my life spent my days
Escaping the creator, seedy as a man
Who disappears from his tricks
Now I ache at the strange
Creation, mine, which like women
Look new in the Court of God

This poem starts with the narrator bowing out, absenting herself occasioned by the presence of the law. Howe's most recent book of essays, *The Winter Sun*, begins, 'Since early adolescence I have wanted to live the life of a poet. What this meant to me was a life outside the law; it would include disobedience and uprootedness.' On the one hand, that law is likely to mean the legal system of the country; in Howe's case, that of the United States. As she notes elsewhere, her father was a Harvard law professor and activist, and activism was in her blood. On the other hand, that law might also have meant the kinds of religious laws or mores which Howe more than once has baulked at. These laws have affected the narrator for such a long time that she has simply given in – she will pay up and leave. It is not the hardship as much as the duration which has had its effect.

The poem then offers an absence that is also a presence. The narrator voluntarily absents herself from the presence of the creator. This creator is seedy because he is a *deus absconditus*, whose presence is a kind of trickery, the kind of demiurge creator of so much early Greek philosophy. There is, however, equally little salvation in the creation that the narrator has occasioned. It is strange, which Howe emphasises in the line-ending caesura that splits the adjective 'strange' from its noun, 'Creation'. This noun is then followed by the possessive pronoun, 'mine', whose stress also emphasises its alterity from the Creator. Howe compounds the alterity by attaching it to 'women'. And these are women who 'look new in the Court of God'. Their presence, itself, suggests a newness, which sets them apart. Even though their gender is rooted in the creation of Eve, women have been absent enough that their presence in God's economy is still a novelty. The 'Court of God' is a space into which Howe pours ethical and social entities, such as the law and feminism.

Presence in absence is revelation. The theologian Christoph Schwöbel states that 'Trying to know God apart from God's revelation is to attempt the impossible because it ignores the fact that God's self-revelation is the only condition for the possibility of knowing God.' In 'The Contemporary Logos', Howe comments, 'The facing of what is in front of you, by sorting out what is behind, goes into the careful syntactic processing of a sentence.' What is immediate and immanent 'in front of you' reveals the absent and transcendent through the immanence. What is behind the immanent then needs to be 'sorted out'. This 'sorting out' implies the incarnation. As Gelpi puts it, in discussing Howe's poem 'NOVEMBER THE NINTH' from her collection 1995 *O'Clock,* 'the resolution to the mystery of life and death somehow lay in the passion of Jesus'. And Gelpi quotes the following lines from that poem, 'But the salt in one single drop / off the chest of Jesus – well, let's follow // Tintoretto to that taste – / where the real is hidden in the paint'. For Howe, the real is 'hidden' in the syntactic processing of the sentence. For Tintoretto, it is the paint that hides in the surface texture and making of the art. For Gelpi, Howe's resolves the mystery of life and death in that 'somehow'. This indicates Howe's resolutely unafraid attitude to uncertainty and fluidity in religion as life.

Gelpi contrasts Fanny Howe's conversion to Catholicism with Susan's Protestantism, 'nonconformist and individualist and antinomian'. In Fanny Howe's incarnational, Catholic theology, Christ's assumption of human-

ity is salvific and redemptive. The differences between the two poets are summed up in lines from the poem 'SUNDAYED', also from *O'Clock,* 'The avant garde worships history, the others choose mystery. So far, God, this may be my last book of unreconstructed poetry.' 'Sunday' is turned into a verb, and not only that, it is turned an active verb whose action conveys change. Sunday is not only the day of rest but also the day of resurrection. 'Unreconstructed' seems rather enigmatic. Does Howe mean a poetry that reaches back to a kind of atavism, a primal or even simple kind of religiousness? If so, such reaching back posits its own dangers. However, as we have seen, Howe is unafraid to face down the dilemmas her work creates. Here she embraces 'the others [who] choose mystery.'

That choice of mystery suggests that Howe's personal theology points towards the apophatic. The apophatic states that it is possible to say what God is not, but it is not possible to say what God is. In poem twelve, in the sequence 'Far and Away' from *The Lyrics* (2007), Howe comments 'What is a poet but a person… Without pretension of knowing / Anything, driven by the lyric's / Quest for rest that never / (God willing) will be found?'

The Lyrics, Howe's fourteenth book, crystallizes much of the restlessness that her work espouses; absence and erasure are key to its themes. Howe explicitly rejects a 'foundational' knowledge, i.e., the sense of a fixed point from which thoughts, ideas, perceptions might arise. The poet's engagement with the lyric in itself militates against that kind of knowledge. Howe almost defines the apophatic, as 'Writing the name "God" poses a problem since an image of God…, can only be empty, negative, *not* sayable. Indeed, rituals and devotional objects serve the purpose of reminding us that named things are not God.' Elsewhere, for example, Howe identifies the Q with 'the Quidam, Whoever, the unknown one' who might actually be a witness. Such statements take us back, yet again, to that being rooted in absence. There is matter but it is the product of deceptions and ambivalences.

Howe's restlessness is pointed up by Romana Huk. Huk looks at what she calls, after St Edith Stein, Howe's use of a 'single liturgy'. The single liturgy is composed of contradictory elements and modes that modernity has tended to keep separate. Stein points, in particular, to 'daily work and prayer'. Howe's single liturgy depends on unravelling what she refers to in her poetry as 'forged' unifiers. She clearly intends for us to read both senses of the word 'forged': the 'made' and the 'falsely representing'. This allows otherness to stand, as well encountering a realistic 'confusion' between differing constituents of the world outside self.

The 'realistic "confusion"' may involve writing as a kind of bricolage. On one level, the yoking of disparate elements can lead to the charge of randomness. The writing becomes aleatory, one manifestation of a consciousness after another. Poems start from one point and then move 'out' to their always provisional and contingent conclusion. On another level, this unravelling and allowing otherness to stand might be one reason why Howe's poetry is often associated with objectivism. Fiona McMahon sums up objectivism as 'affirming the need for a greater attentiveness to the language of poetry and an acute awareness of the perceptual realities that shape one's immediate circumstances'. 'Greater attentiveness' can lead to a furious concentration on what the poem *can* do in its prolonged negotiation with language.

Part of that furious concentration is shown in the *O'Clock* collection. The cover of the British edition shows two young girls, Irish-dancing on a wooden floor inside a large tent. It is evidently a competition, because the girls are wearing labels with numbers on them. The girls are concentrating on the instant because of the competition. The poems in *O'Clock* show 'acute awareness' of 'one's immediate circumstances' in their titles which are usually the time from the twenty-four-hour clock or a date written in capital letters. Clair Wills suggests that 'Time is collapsed into the instantaneous moment, even as it is clear that the poems themselves cannot be produced within this moment... or what Howe elsewhere calls, after Coleridge, "the contemporaneous moment."'

Howe's poems also reflect how traditional Christian concepts may actually offer more absences than they offer certainties. These spaces become vessels into which Howe places questioning which reaches deep into Howe's own beliefs. This is a complete poem from the *Q* sequence:

Heaven has been my nation-state
safe sanctuary from the law
or else the production of hate and bread is not
increasing

At least I know my tradition is among the contradictions

And rests upon a time
as close to never-was as anything can be

but still a story of something that almost came to be
the never-quite-but-hinted-at
attention of a Thee

The unmetered verse and the lack of punctuation emphasise the 'contemporaneous now' in structure. Lack of punctuation melds the syntax of each line through and against the line breaks and acts as a circularity in the poem itself. The last line connects to the first. Lack of punctuation softens the very definite line endings, and the separations of stanzas, although line groupings would possibly be a better term. The first line has a defiant quality to it. 'Has been' works to suggest that Heaven might both still be her nation-state, and that it was once but is no longer. We might also wonder in what sense 'Heaven' has existence as a nation-state except in a metaphysical way. The next line might suggest continuation of the state described in the first line and is equally abrupt and defiant. We might wish to ask which 'law' it is that Heaven is a safe sanctuary from. And who is it that is producing the 'hate and bread'? Is this production internal to Howe? Does Heaven protect her from herself?

These questions seem encouraged by the rest of the poem. Not only is the narrator/Howe's tradition among the contradictions; those contradictions are emphasised on the page by the line spaces before and after, and embedded in the syntax. However, the contradictions are located in a moment that seems so liminal, so 'close to never-was', that its very existence can be questioned. And yet, even if that moment feels nebulous, the tradition is still a 'story of something'. That 'something', too, is reduced to a possibility swamped by the 'almost came to be'. That something is defined in the final line as the 'attention of a Thee'. But even here, that attention and its agent are subverted by 'the never-quite-but-hinted-at'. It is as if the Thee and his attentions are like a game of Chinese Whispers. The 'Thee' is clearly religious, clearly, in fact, Christian, and our attention is drawn to it by the capitalization. The indefinite article, however, skews 'Thee' away from precision and its own incarnational in/finitude; this is one 'Thee' among many.

This text's trajectory of ideas develops within an almost infinite regress of uncertainty. The lack of punctuation might encourage us to see the ideational structure of the poem as fluid and permeable but held within Wills/Coleridge's 'contemporaneous now'. However, the idea that Heaven is a nation-state and therefore a sanctuary seems fatally undermined by the imprecisions of the final five lines. What might seem to be bounded as a nation-state and a sanctuary is actually found to be an absence. That absence revolves around the peculiar axle that is 'the contradictions' of line four. What finally seems certain is that all these things are write-able. The poet can work out in black and white of these contradictions. The poem is an offering from within differing perspectives, theological, temporal, activist, projectivist – of all the tensions these perspectives evoke.

Howe has continued to explore these perspectives into the twentieth century. Her volume *The Lyrics* (2007) starts with a sequence called 'Forty Days'. The Christian resonances are clear. However, as Howe would know, forty days in Christian mythology does not only apply to Christ's time in the wilderness before he starts his ministry. Forty days was the time when Christ deliberately placed himself in the way of temptation. Forty was also the number of days between Christ's resurrection and his ascension, the length of the Easter season in the Christian year. The first two sections of Howe's poem are as follows:

It's the summer solstice
The day the darkening begins

If I keep walking west
I can precede this time again

In a year. Not much stamina
Foot-shoes sore

Passing war after war
Between ad-nauseam errors

Unsure of which was after
And which is before.

If I can just keep walking
It will not be now
But next
If I can say with the gravity

That troubles the sea you'll see
I will come to that day

Now I can taste its goodness
Without me

Even though this poem is delineated by its section number 1, Howe, again, dispenses with most of the punctuation. What underpins, or perhaps undermines, these content units is the use of conditional clauses beginning with 'If I...'. Thus the forty days are a kind of temptation as the narrator sees her progress as conditional on her ability simply to carry on. In her essay 'The Contemporary Logos', Howe sees such situations as very much the situation of Beckett's characters who are aligned with the attitudes espoused by Simone Weil. Howe writes,

> When words are mouthed through Beckett's characters – centuries after the crucifixion of Christ – affliction, silence and history have torn them from an origin... 'This is the point in affliction where we are no longer able to bear either that it should go on or that we should be delivered from it,' writes Weil. ('I can't go on, I go on,' writes Beckett.)

In *Molloy*, Beckett writes,

> And having heard, or more probably read somewhere, in the days when I thought I would be well advised to educate myself, or amuse myself, or stupefy myself, or kill time, that when a man in a forest thinks he is going forward in a straight line, in reality he is going in a circle, I did my best to go in a circle, hoping this way to go in a straight line.

Howe's poem from *The Lyrics* uses a number of conditional clauses. These conditionals echo Beckett's purposes, 'to education/amuse/stupefy/kill time'. Beckett lines them up with his 'I thought I would' in order to rationalise his actions; his volition 'in the days' in the past. And Beckett's writing is heavily punctuated, perhaps to mimic the breathing of his protagonist. Howe's line breaks have, as we have seen, that slightly end-stopped, halting quality. Where Howe's persona is walking to 'precede this time again' so that 'It will not be now / but next', Molloy *hopes* that he is walking in a straight line by doing his best to walk in a circle. Both trajectories feel 'torn' from their origins by the 'affliction, silence and history' that Howe ascribes to the words that Beckett's characters

mouth. The *telos* in Howe's poem is that there is a goodness outside the narrator. This *telos* has its own essence, almost an agency that is not willed in the being of the narrator. In the midst of this personal sense of volition and destiny rejected or accepted, history lies in the 'war after war / Between ad-nauseam errors'. These lines were written in the aftermath of 9/11 and the Bush wars that followed. The nausea that these wars create must be overcome by a goodness that can be tasted aside from the singular agency of the taster.

Early in her writing, Howe recognised the ethical implications of a universal singularity that is both centripetal and centrifugal. In 'Robeson Street', a sequence from 1985, and which is based on the mixed-race area in Boston in which she lived, Howe wrote, 'Mixed clouds are more propitious than fleece / and the poor who are occluded / and stationary will tell the true story'. This seems to refer to the aporia in society in which the poor have been occluded. Howe shows the ethical nature of the narrative with the adjectives 'propitious' and 'true'. We might suggest that the centripetal/centrifugal dynamic occurs in exactly that stationary occlusion of the poor who will tell the narrative that is true. And this message supports the initial metaphor of the mixed clouds being more propitious than the 'pure' fleece. Again, this latter image plunges us back into the iconography of Christianity, which, we have seen, Howe often views with considerable ambivalence.

This essay has tried to establish the ways in which the American poet Fanny Howe has approached the idea of aporia. This aporia may be both the site of an absence but also the place out of which the need to search may arise. That search, in Howe's case, involves, at its most intimate, the ways in which poetry may reveal God in his absence. The search may also reveal the way in which humans are absent to each other. In both cases, these absences are explored in poetry which refuses to ameliorate those absences. The poetry does not offer solutions, but may simply pose the questions in better ways. However, 'better' does not for Howe mean simplicity or increased explicitness. Howe's poetry is not 'public' poetry in the ways in which, say, Robert Lowell's poetry was seen as 'public', addressing national issues such as the Vietnam war. Howe's poetry explores aporia, and the relation of the centripetal to the centrifugal by acknowledging that surface facility will not suffice. And that very acknowledgement has made her poetry some of the most interesting and demanding of the twenty-first century.

Headstones

JOSEPH MINDEN

Lights up. What light. A Malaysian number. Mina. Ordnance Survey crystals. Mells, obviously. Catkins hazing April, Somerset from branches parting. Suddenly past Lutyens, street view retrospect. Side-struck with morning sun, thudding through wild garlic in the valley, footholds of old sockets in stone. Close to wet stone, the smell of moss, of earth still moist in shade. Volume of breath. I spun round in the clearing and was struck again, concussed by a passing cloud. A Sopwith Camel over Cadbury Camp. The drifty hummocks they say were Camelot. The melting parallelogram of the Quantocks where we broke down.

*

Fragrances like melodies, orange lanterns leaching from my temples, the street trembling. Once, a letter would have taken four months to travel from London to Penang. Faster by opium clipper. A bottleneck of shipping lanes dotted through the Straits of Malacca, becoming a black glut. MALAY STATES in a banner across the landmass. Straits Settlements in small script in the sea. Mina in the George Town Festival office. Smoking a clove cigarette in the evening shade. Watching emails arrive in her inbox. Pressing delete. I shut my eyes and stand next to her for a second on that first night, in her hands. Blissfully passive.

*

One day we drove directly south, bypassing Shaftesbury, Blandford Forum, Bere Regis, and shot the arrow of our bounden sight right through the stately arch of Durdle Door. The breeze blew over frozen Tyneham. Coffee dripped in an earthenware pot. Mina walked back to the car, walnuts falling near the house, peaches closing over the claws of the boughs. At Montacute, Dicken looked up from the till, his eyes an explosion of irises. Agnosia of the beds. No forms but fading blues, yellows, creams, apricots, pinks, mauves, reds. White and obscure lenses hurrying up. The slow expansion of the reds. All flower and faceless.

*

Jason is off to the Front. Will I go with him? I remember that school trip so well, press-ganged by the luminous white graves. Then broken up and rearranged like earth, like cloud. German remains shovelled into a pit at Langemark. A grief not given room. A grief for which power could not stake out the relief of space. My teacher an absurd and statuesque ghoul among the accusatory oaks, the thousands of names. And it was the whites in the sky overhead that didn't move. The squat blocks in the ground began to drift. What were they teaching? Of course I'll go. Rolling round Picardy in a Mini listening to Lloyd Cole sounds like heaven.

*

MacDonald Gill at Pitzhanger Manor. A room full of low chatter like a sky full of Sopwith Camels. The Empire Marketing Board's first poster, Highways of Empire. MALAY STATES in a banner across the landmass. Straits Settlements in small script in the sea. Mina, lighting up. Then, distinct and bright white in the centre of the gallery, a War Graves Commission headstone. Gill's crisp lettering. A SOLDIER OF THE GREAT WAR KNOWN UNTO GOD. How many rows of those calling from Flanders and the Somme? Their glowing, solitary counterparts shining like mushrooms in English graveyards.

*

The majority are Portland stone but some are Hopton Wood limestone from Derbyshire, where they quarried to meet excess demand. Near Middleton, there are remnants of broken headstones in the walls. I stepped across my dreams up to the pile of concrete. White chips in miniature drifts. Needles in piles. Jason called back to say turn left at the end of the lane there, descend soundlessly into a sudden fir plantation, fall asleep in the front seats in April, May, June. Some month from the freshness of the year. I looked up from the jump leads to find myself flying over Tyne Cot with a pouch full of milk teeth for the boys.

*

The truth is not a headstone but a pit. Blank earth in the hollows of the body. Uncle Roy, escaping from a sinking submarine off Bastia, dying of his dreams in Rome. Hidden in the soil are small and loving models, holy sites plundered by soldiers in bright colours, the purples and yellows of spring, the postures of infancy crystallised as toys. What is remembered is what is forgotten, splitting from itself, turning in a different direction in the valley. I thought it was white as snow but it was red as blood, hundreds of white teeth turning in the eye of a red flower, whiteness misting to an uncountable array of red flowers.

*

The glacial segments of the fillets bristled as Jason unwrapped them from the waxed paper. Red and yellow light of nighttime. Mina and I walking like ghosts over frozen furrows in Blenheim Park hours before, steam billowing. Strange how I see it. Staring in from December darkness, breath wreathing my head. Me and Jason, marinaded in yellow light, talking by the sink. Fenugreek, cumin, fennel seeds spitting in a dented pan. The window frame buckling and curving, becoming circular. The ground loosening, tilting, becoming water. The house lurching, distending, becoming a clipper bound for Canton with its cargo of opium.

*

It is only in my memory that I feel so alone. In reality, Mina was waiting at the airport, standing with me in the queue for food, time flowing over the weir. A row of cypresses against a red wall, its roots in our veins. Nepenthe. Helen relieving Telemachus and Menelaus of all memory of the war. Lin Zexu and Joseph of Arimathea holding hands on Glastonbury Tor, the drug pouring into the sea. All the solace in Benares, Patna, Malwa, burning in a meadow of trenches. Daoguang waking up to rumours of pests in metal ships from the West Ocean. Foxed by the size of his own empire. Where, in fact, was England?

*

Our stomachs were the lure of blankness. Ice and condensed milk browning with Malacca sugar. Pits of green noodles. A wound in slow motion walking through Bristol, Dover, Liverpool to the water. Up Mincing Lane and Exchange Alley. Sniffing at the threshold of Garraway's Coffee House. Drifting over remote earthworks, the infinite promise of a moment in time, the sky when you are high on a hill, infested with Sopwith Camels. Textile mills in the Midlands collapsing, slave ships repurposed as opium boats, the familiarity of the witch vanishing over the low wall on her broomstick, rounding the headland in an eggshell.

*

The row of cypresses, the red wall. There was an old love. The same love, in fact. A seam under the veil of the soil. But is there a brother to mourn in that specific grave? Uncle Roy, waking up from a sinking submarine to find himself falling from a window, already wrapped in his funeral shroud. Warmth weakens from the bedsheets like a fragrance. The row of cypresses. The red wall. I am clawing the ground, unable to explain the objects turning up in my hands. Underneath is one growing mouth, one building scream. But the noise is aborted, compressed into these teeth, these plastic toys, these flowers.

*

A whale vertebra from Zoology. A dip circle from the Whipple. A page of Southern Beech specimens from the Botanical Gardens. Rubbish rattling around among roots. I walked to the train station and the jungle went changelessly to ruins. Fussell's factory in Mells. Mina laughing through coins and portals of light. Jason rounding the corner in his Mini. Provisions spilt onto a checked cloth, demolished on a green in East Coker. I'd barely swallowed but I opened up again. Not the talking. Fish heads threw off their sauce and got up to levitate out. Oysters sped from omelettes. Coffees punched holes downwards out of time.

*

There are no headstones for what is under the ground, only for what is held at the surface. The place where my foot meets the gravel, where the plane hits the runway, where the sun touches the water. I will not call them by their names, their names cannot reach them. The whiteness of their faces mists into a red field. I am under the earth. This cemetery in which I stand at dusk, the sunset I drive off in: complications in the soil. Root, bone, scrap chandeliers. There are no headstones for what is under the name. A name, like a photograph, proof that memory fails. Roy, for example. Mina. There, that will do.

*

The night will be cool, hardening into winter. I'll stumble over a prone lad and go off, chilled. The ferry will be quiet, the light yellow. We'll be in Ypres on November 11 for the last post, eating eels full of spine out of a horribly thick cream sauce in the square. The first night we'll sleep near Albert, in the heart of the Somme. The second we'll spend in Poperinge, gateway to the battlefields of the Ypres Salient, billet for British troops. After dinner, I'll suddenly stand up, needing to breathe. I'll walk out into the square, take out my phone and dial a number. The bell will start ringing. Without warning, the square will flood.

*

Thousands of poppies appear and blossom into bulbs of smoke. Each bulb soon falls out of shape, rising, distending, blowing off. Through the haze, it becomes clear that there are also thousands of figures lying there beneath, blissed out beyond recollection, complete as stones. Understated bulbs of smoke flower from their mouths, carrying care, rephrasing memories as wordless dreams. Unthinkable objects. A smoke that freezes briefly in the reds of poppies, drifting up in thousands of trails like the aftermath of a bombardment. Others in the sky, drifting in giant shade like blimps, discover teeth, plastic toys, flowers.

*

The exhibition opened this evening. *Discovery*'s bell rang in celebration. I thought about Mina, what she was doing. I mean, she would have been asleep. But now. Early hours here. She'll have woken. She'll be walking through the streets before the heat, past the heritage pinks, blues, yellows of the shophouses. Picking up breakfast, her face gone. I walked home slowly after the guests had left, out beneath the MacDonald Gill domes. Lensfield Avenue deserted. On Parker's Piece, the lime trees trembled. In Reality Checkpoint's lemony glow, an enamoured soul sucked on their lover's neck. Flecks of scarlet on ice-white.

Reviews

Making the World Bearable

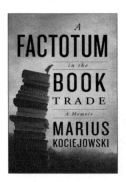

Marius Kociejowski, *A Factotum in the Book Trade*
(Biblioasis: Windsor, Ontario) £13.99
Reviewed by Alberto Manguel

For about three years, during my adolescence, I worked as a bookseller in an English-German bookshop in Buenos Aires. I don't think I could do it again. Especially not in an antiquarian bookshop where books come with what my grandmother called, when speaking about certain doubtful characters, 'a history'. Now, once I have a book in my hands, especially one with 'a history', I am loath to give it up. I'm less of a book collector than a book hoarder and my motto is that of Polonius: 'Neither borrower nor lender be'.

So it is with admiration and respect that I started to read this memoir by the legendary Marius Kociejowski. He's a year younger than I am, but oh, so much more knowledgeable and wiser. Apparently, he has done everything: journeyed into the wilds of the Near East, and written about those journeys; composed volumes of very decent poetry and read entire libraries of the stuff; become familiar with most of the bookselling gang in Canada and England; chinwagged with the Mafia in Naples; studied for fun and profit the writings of Wittgenstein, Tycho Brahe, Robert Louis Stevenson, Zoroaster and Nietzsche, to name but a few. He also bought and sold antiquarian books.

This last sentence, today, can seemingly only be spoken in the past tense. Though many antiquarian booksellers continue to exercise their arduous trade in spite of contrary winds, sometimes hitching their craft onto virtual ocean liners, sometimes sailing through cyberspace singlehandedly, their task has become increasingly difficult. Knowlegeable customers (we are told) are now a species close to extinction, and libraries (we are also told) no longer require books of paper and ink but can feed, like the chameleon Love, on air. Kociejowski explains his pursuits this way: 'The world is getting faster and faster and our evolutionary development cannot keep pace, and with the imperative that we move faster still, what has happened is that there has been a shift from active knowledge, which demands of us that we aggressively *pursue* answers, to passive knowledge, whereby we are *fed* information.' His own vocation is not a yes-or-no catechism but closer to the rabbinical method of answering a question with another question.

Thus Kociejowski's memoir trails from one question to the next, from one encounter to the following illuminating encounter, from one uneasy step in the professional bookseller's career to another, uneasier step. Kociejowski divides book collectors into magpies and hawks. Magpies, he says, 'collect whatever looks attractive to them at the time'. Hawks 'collect books with a clear focus'. Like Kociejowski, I'm unsurprisingly a magpie. In the life of a magpie there are no certainties.

Kociejowski gives invaluable observations and tips for anyone interested in the antiquarian book trade, some culled from colleagues and acquaintances, others from his own experience: 'It is one of those bibliographical mysteries that books bound in green cloth are often the most difficult to sell.' 'A book collector will think irrationally.' 'A good book is a book one has a use for.' 'The term "book collector" was invented by people who don't buy books to describe people who do.' 'All systems fail for lack of space.' 'There's something oddly pleasurable about packing a book – it's an unwinding of sorts, an expression of contentment' (a morbid contentment, I might add from personal experience.) And this, my own life's motto: 'Security shoos away adventure'.

His quotations shed light on my own. One of my favourites is Borges's definition of the effect of art: 'The imminence of a revelation that does not take place.' I now realize, thanks to Kociejowski, that it's a translation of Stevenson's observation: 'It has the essence of all art, an unexplored imminent significance.' Borges knew Stevenson by heart but he never revealed this secret source.

Kociejowski drops names of poets he knew or heard

read like crumbs from a greedy child's cookie: Ted Hughes, George Barker, Amy Clampitt, Roy Fisher, Tony Harrison, David Gascoyne, Sorley MacLean, Geoffrey Hill, W.S. Graham, Robert Creeley, John Ashbery, Philip Larkin (in whose poems, Kociejowski says, 'Despair becomes its own comfort zone'), obliging me to get out a pencil and jot down the names of the ones I didn't know.

Kociejowski has some of the best anecdotes I've ever heard, many merely entertaining, even trivial but, as he wisely tells us: 'Triviality can be, on occasion, a good indicator of depth of feeling between two people'. Some are delightful gems, like the one about George Lawson (of Bertram Rota, 'one of the last old establishments, dynastic and oxygenless') who left money to a giraffe in Edinburgh Zoo 'because it reminded him of his wife who was tall'. Or the one about the bookish Sergey Savitsky who, while working on a remote station in Antarctica, stabbed his colleague Oleg Beloguzov in the chest with a kitchen knife because Beloguzov 'kept revealing the endings of books from the station before Savitsky had a chance to read them'. (Bully for Savitsky, I say.) Some of the anecdotes are strictly bibliophilic but become epiphanies in the light of Kociejowski's comments. For instance, he tells us (and who am I to doubt Kociejowski) that the first non-religious book printed in Malta in Maltese orthography in 1846 (up to then Malta had employed Arabic script) is *Il Haya u il Vinturi ta' Robinson Krusoe*. 'A solitary man', Kociejowski observes, 'on a solitary island in a solitary language.'

As in the best of memoirs, I come across common friends: *PN Review* editor Michael Schmidt; William Blisset (who when mistaken for the poet Bill Bisset responded 'There's an l of a difference between us'); William Hoffer, the Vancouver bookseller who strong-armed Leonard Cohen out of his shop; the undeservedly forgotten Canadian novelist Margaret Laurence; the poet Eric Ormsby.

Towards the end of his memoir, Marius Kociejowski says that 'sometimes I entertain the notion my books will continue, together, without me'. I share the same notion. I've heard tell that when a beekeeper dies, someone must go tell the bees that their keeper is dead. Since then I've wished that when I die, someone will do the same for me and tell my books that I will not come back, and that they should stay together to continue without me their generous friendship. The friendship of books lends some sense to the madness of the world. In Kociejowski's words, this is part of those 'small rituals of solitude, which makes the clawing world bearable'.

The Deserted Plantation

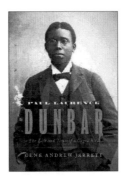

Gene Andrew Jarrett, *Paul Laurence Dunbar: The life and times of a caged bird* (Princeton) £28
Reviewed by James Campbell

Paul Laurence Dunbar (1872–1906) was two different poets and two different men. One of the poets wrote stately, well-formed verses that risked sounding out of date even in the 1890s, when Dunbar was in demand for recitals in both the United States and England. Some lines from 'Harriet Beecher Stowe' give the flavour:

> Her message, Freedom's clear reveille, swept
>   From heedless hovel to complacent throne,
>   Command and prophecy were in the tone
>   And from its sheath the sword of justice leapt.

It was another sort of poem that audiences came to hear, though Dunbar felt patronized and feared he was mistreating his gift by catering for the demand. This was his Negro dialect verse, related – though only superficially – to the commercially successful minstrel shows, to what were known, among black and white alike, as 'coon songs' (and, in the century after, to the blues). Dunbar wrote numerous poems in dialect. Many are profound and poignant, such as 'When Dey 'Listed Colored Soldiers', written from the point of view of a mother whose son has been conscripted to fight in the Civil War; or the brilliant 'The Deserted Plantation', which gives a picture of desolation when the slaves have departed in the years after Emancipation, a loneliness felt not only in the fields but in the big house, too. An example of the wit that amused listeners is found in 'Soliloquy of a Turkey'. As Christmas approaches, the bird senses that recent improvements in living conditions are not what they seem:

> Folks is go'gin' me wid goodies, an' dey's treatin' me wid caih,
>   An' I's fat in spite of all dat I kin do.
> I's mistrustful of de kin'ness dat's erroun' me evahwhaih,
>   Fu' it's jes' too good, an frequent, to be true.

Dunbar died of tuberculosis at the age of thirty-three, four years younger than Robert Burns at the time of his death – another ambidextrous poet whose work in dialect has proved more enduring than his well-ordered manner. There have been others, including Sterling Brown, born in Washington DC within the lifetime of Dunbar, and, in Scotland, Robert Garioch and Hugh MacDiarmid. In general, when the dialect poems find favour, it is unusual in the career of a successful poet to see the 'straight' verse keeping up.

Dunbar's mother, Matilda, had been a slave in Kentucky. A photograph of 1890 in Gene Andrew Jarrett's excellent biography shows an attractive woman with bright eyes, dressed in special-occasion crinoline with ornamental cane and gloves. She recalled 'kind and indulgent' owners, who leased her, as was the custom, to work on neighbouring plantations, even as a seven- and eight-year-old.

By the time Paul was born, the Dunbars were living in Dayton, Ohio, where Paul attended Central High School. In one of many surprising details, Jarrett describes the friendship he formed there with the Wright Brothers, Orville and Wilbur, who later built the world's first viable aeroplane. Class photographs show Dunbar as the only black student. He was an outstanding one. His debut, *Oak and Ivy*, published locally when he was twenty, displayed 'a diverse array of poetic styles', Jarrett writes. Dunbar was proud of his prosodic skills, and affronted when they were insufficiently appreciated.

With *Oak and Ivy*, Dunbar's voice was nevertheless at large, and publication occurred regularly thereafter. It was at about the same time that the unpleasant side of his character began to show. He inherited his father's weakness for liquor, and developed a taste for fast women. These traits existed side by side with a yearning for respectable living. In 1895, he began a correspondence with Alice Moore, not yet twenty, from New Orleans. In an archaic precursor of today's online dating, the couple got to know each other through letters and the occasional photograph. Whereas he was dark, she was light-complexioned, which, says Jarrett, 'captivated him... . [W]ithin many African American communities, social stature rose in proportion to the lightness of skin color.' Miss Moore was cultured and intelligent. She had just published her own first book, and would later gain a modest reputation as a journalist. Her response to Dunbar's urgent epistles was instinctively hesitant. Even before they met in person, he expressed 'a tinge of jealousy' over the fond dedication of her book to an unnamed friend (displeasure came in the form of a quote from *Hamlet*). He warned her that he could be 'agreeable or disagreeable', adding, 'I can be the latter with a vengeance'.

And so it proved. Eventually, Alice agreed to marry him, but apparently not to sleep with him before the wedding day. Drunk one night in New York, he raped her, necessitating medical attention over many weeks (but not causing an annulment of the planned union). Often on tour, he pursued other women, and let Alice know. Shortly after she accepted his proposal, he was on his way to England for a series of readings. 'The girls here are not only mildly seductive but aggressive', he told his fiancée. When she was slow to reply, he would switch tones: 'Oh darling, darling life of my life!... I would rather be your captive than another woman's king', and so on.

Dunbar's recitals were sometimes cancelled because of what Jarrett calls 'excessive drinking and inebriation'. He assaulted Alice and kept alive a passion for an old flame, Rebekah. In addition to personal failings, he was increasingly unwell, and from the end of the century until his death in 1906 would never be properly well again.

Yet the words continued to come – poetry, fiction, libretti, essays. A photograph in this well-illustrated biography shows a huge crowd – standing room only – listening to the slight young man give a recital in his home town, Dayton, in 1903. In an interview with a New York newspaper, Dunbar made a statement that displays the depth of his insight into American poetry, and the society that produces it:

It appears to me that that is not negro poetry only which is written by negroes, but all that is written by whites who have received their inspiration from negro life. The races have acted and reacted on each other. The white man who, as a child, was suckled at the breast of the black mammy has received the strongest influence of his life, perhaps, from the African race. Why, the white people in the south talk like us – they have imported many of our words into the language – and you know they act like us.

This anticipates the literary procedures and opinions of certain twentieth-century writers, including William Faulkner, Albert Murray, and above all Ralph Ellison: 'I tell white kids that instead of talking about black men in a white world or black men in a white society, they should be asking themselves how black they are....'

It was the title poem of one of Dunbar's later books, *When Malindy Sings*, that first brought him to my attention – but in the form of a song. Abbey Lincoln recorded a shortened version in 1961 with an illustrious ensemble including Coleman Hawkins and Max Roach. The poem, written before the recording era, at a time when public appreciation of African American entertainment was mostly restricted to music hall and minstrelsy, is an announcement and celebration of the instinct and urgency of black music, qualities that would power a range of forms in the century to come, from blues to jazz, gospel to R&B, and carry them all over the world:

G'way an' quit dat noise, Miss Lucy –
    Put dat music book away;
What's de use to keep on tryin'?
    Ef you practise twell you're gray,
You cain't sta't no notes a-flyin'
    Lak de ones dat rants and rings
F'om de kitchen to de big woods
    When Malindy sings.

Paul Laurence Dunbar is thoroughly researched and elegantly written. Mr Jarrett sensitively outlines the conditions that contributed to his subject's bad behaviour, without excusing it or shying away from its effects on others. He leaves the reader eager for more information about Alice Moore (later Alice Dunbar Nelson), who outlived her first husband by almost thirty years. My sole criticism of this handsome book is the absence of a simple bibliography.

Lowell's missing line-ends

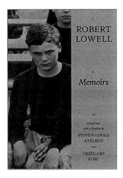

Robert Lowell, *Memoirs*, eds. Steven Gould Axelrod and
Grzegorz Kosc (Faber) £40
Reviewed by Tony Roberts

Robert Giroux, famed editor and Lowell's friend, pub-
lished a valuable selection, *Robert Lowell: Collected Prose*,
which I have had at hand for more than thirty years. Now
Steven Gould Axelrod and Grzegorz Kosc, veteran Lowell
critics, have applied serious scholarship to papers housed
in Harvard University's Houghton Library and elsewhere,
to offer a comprehensive compilation. The editors' brief
is to establish the case for his standing in prose – to 'dis-
play another dimension of Lowell's artistry' – which was
first evident from the extract '91 Revere Street' in *Life Stud-
ies* (1959). To support that end, each section has also an
introduction, a note on the texts and very many corrective
footnotes.

The result is a meticulously edited volume, which great-
ly expands on Giroux's book, centrally in bringing out
Lowell's substantial, incomplete autobiography begun
during rehabilitation after a bipolar episode, which was
the source of much of the highly influential *Life Studies*.

In 'My Autobiography' we are treated to a version of the
unlovable young Lowell, his hysterical, 'Napoleonic'
mother and a father whose 'soul went underground'. Low-
ell writes with brio and not without humour: the gener-
ous deployment of the Lowellian triplets, those
surprising, surreal adjectives ('Through a wide-open win-
dow and blowing organdy, drowsed the tepid, seedy, ele-
phantine air of an April afternoon in Washington') and
clever thumbnail sketches: his talkative grandmother and
her friend who 'never sounded like poultry', or the hus-
band for whom 'children were a hallucination'.

Being Lowell, everything reprises the nation's history
and his family's role in it. The heavily wood-stained water
is 'almost as red as the jackets of silver-wigged Colonial
officials'. At the Smithsonian, 'We passed by Cousin Cas-
sie James's 1840s slippers; we passed by Dolley Madison's
inaugural dress that Mother, a newly elected Colonial
Dame, was collaborating on.' The life is all fearfully priv-
ileged and the relationships dysfunctional. Where the
allusions are not historical they are literary: 'I would pass
away the sick hours looking at Raphael's *Portinari* and
the madonnas of Carlo Dolci in Mother's scrapbook.'

Lowell's hostility to his parents is more pronounced in
Memoirs than in his poetry. He acknowledged in one inter-
view adopting 'a fairly gentle style' for the latter, describ-
ing it six years later as 'a style I thought I had discovered

in Flaubert, one that used images and ironic or amusing
particulars'. Yet poetry enters *Memoirs* as the 'life preserv-
er' and the 'battering ram against everything and every-
body that puzzled me or seemed indifferent or critical'.

Having the autobiography inevitably invites compari-
sons between the prose and the poetry of *Life Studies*. The
prose supplies the image or the moment; the poem crys-
tallises it: '"But I don't want to go anywhere; I want to go
to *Rock*!" That's how I would stop conversation, when my
mother and father talked about trips to Paris, Puget
Sound, Mattapoisett... ...anywhere!' This becomes

> 'I won't go with you. I want to stay with Grandpa!'
> That's how I threw cold water
> on my Mother and Father's
> watery martini pipe dreams at Sunday dinner.
> ... Fontainebleau, Mattapoisett, Puget Sound...'

The first line tightens the desire; the fourth adds a deli-
cious whimsy; 'Paris' becomes the evocative 'Fontaine-
bleau'.

After the family debacles and Lowell's accounts of
struggling through his manic periods, *Memoirs* turns to
the determinedly personal literary portraits. In his *Paris
Review* interview of 1961 Lowell acknowledged, 'Some-
times I wish I did more, but I'm very anxious in criticism
not to do the standard analytical essay. I'd like my essay
to be much sloppier and more intuitive.' In *Memoirs*, he
sees a contrast with Allen Tate's criticism: 'I still have too
little interest in sustained argument, sustained polemic,
to much want to write a critical essay.'

Instead we have these relatively short pieces in which
Lowell reminisces about his mentors (Tate, Ransom,
Ford, Frost, Pound, Eliot, Williams, Warren), writes ele-
gies for his friends Berryman and Jarrell (his 'undertak-
er's pieces') and estimations of younger writers (Sexton,
Plath) and his peers (Arendt), ending with thoughts on
his own 'wayfaring' ('After Enjoying Six or Seven Essays
on Me'). Here we have the clear-eyed anecdotes, shot
through with insight and raffish imagery. One piece on
Pound ends with fine, comical deflation:

> 'I said, "You are one of the few living men who has
> walked through Purgatory." Watching me like a cat, and
> catching my affectation and affection, he answered,
> "Didn't Frost say you'd say anything once for the hell
> of it?"'

There are intimate disclosures and interesting judg-
ments: Eliot's 'influence is everywhere inescapable and
nowhere really usable'; 'Tate sometimes seems a Tennes-
see version of Eliot, so close are their prejudices, so close
are their discoveries'; Ransom is 'the intellectual father
I would have chosen'; the young Jarrell was 'upsettingly
brilliant, precocious, knowing, naïve, and vexing'; 'An
indignant spirit was born in [Berryman]; his life was a
cruel fight to set it free'; Sexton's 'gift was to grip, to give
words to the drama of her personality'; 'language never
dies in [Plath's] mouth'.

For all the sadness in *Memoirs*, it is a life-affirming col-
lection. I am reminded of Jonathan Raban's comment:
'Lowell's laughter, his utterly unpredictable quickness of
mind, his sureness of heart and eye shine through his

prose exactly as they shone in conversation.' To me it is a poet's book, for Lowell proved a master of sifting his prose for its poetic potential. Compression suited him. Once, after writing an obituary, he complained 'I was naked without my line-ends'. *Memoirs* shows, however, just how little the poet needed them. Essential reading.

Something Close to Music

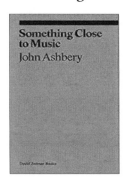

John Ashbery, *Something Close to Music*, edited by Jeffrey Lependorf
(David Zwirner Books) £8.95
Reviewed by Harry Sanderson

Stendhal once said it was it was other arts that taught him the art of writing. I don't know where he said it, only that the film director Robert Bresson quoted him to that effect in an interview, a story Clive James told Peter Porter in an old radio recording. I recount that chain of reception in order to illustrate a principle parallel to Stendhal's own: how works of art press into one another, giving a liquidity to forms often treated as mutually exclusive.

That idea – or is it a process?– is central to John Ashbery's work. Critics have focused on his origins as an art critic, his affinity for music, and his frequent use of ekphrasis, a genre loosely defined as literature responding to works of art. Yet the treatment is often limp for being overly literal, with critics satisfied to point out where his poems refer to paintings. *Something Close to Music,* edited by Jeffrey Lependorf as part of David Zwirner Books's Ekphrasis series, engages Ashbery's process on closer terms by selecting a series of poems, art critical essays and playlists from Ashbery's music collection.

Ashbery constantly framed his art writing as a minor pastime, undertaken to make money while destitute in Paris. In one sense the essays here do play in a minor key: they are brief, colloquial, and almost always begin with a personal anecdote, so that they become something of a diary. Yet they are not minor in the sense of being cursory or effete. In the manner of John Berger and the late Peter Schjeldahl, Ashbery's conversational tone harbours sharp critical insights. Against the consensus that Mapplethorpe is a voyeur of priapic depravity, for example, Ashbery comments that the conditions of his stylised photographs infer a trust between photographer and subject, so that the squalor is only ever supposed. It's an observation that strikes as percipient and novel, delivered with the offhand confidence of an autodidact.

The poems selected were all published after 1987, so as to mirror the essays. In his brief introduction Lependorf focuses on the multiplicity found in Ashbery's work, proposing that 'we can read and think through his poetry in a multitude of ways, drawing different conclusions with each reading'. Yet I find that Ashbery's embrace of the uncertainties of perception renders such a search for conclusions futile. As Ben Lerner has commented, his work 'pins us to the moment of reading and frustrates retrograde interpretive strategies that would stop the flow of language at its source'. The saturation of hypotaxis in the poems only ever offers the sense of semantic coherence, never delivering the content of actual thought. The poem is less a choose-your-own-adventure than a labyrinth of syntax, a quest without treasure. Take this passage from Part III of the long poem *Flow Chart*, which Lependorf extracts:

> No but there is a logic
> to be used in such situations, and only then: a curl of
> smoke or fuzziness in distant trees
> that tempts one down the slope, and sure enough,
> there is a village, festive preparations,
> a votive smile on the face of each inhabitant that lets
> you pass through
> unquestioned.

The negative preposition at the beginning of the sentence suggests a narrative argument, which Ashbery introduces in the 'logic' of his poems, and promises to reveal through the early colon: but the passage never meets meaning, and the story is deferred down towards the village. Always Ashbery propels us towards rhetorical and poetic certainty, with phrases such as 'sure enough' intimating a final coherence – but the solace is always postponed, the journey prolonged, like the visitor tempted along the slope towards the settlement only to pass through unquestioned.

'Considering the temporality of this process – Lerner observes that Ashbery's work 'manages to describe the time of its own reading in the time of its own reading' – it is intuitive for music to have a place in the collection through the five curated playlists interspersed between poems and essays. Ashbery listened to music while he worked, and the recordings here offer a complement to his reading, as well as a concentration of his tastes. Again, the collection allows the music to move through the writing without scaffolding, as Ashbery provides occasional points of contact: one essay on Frank Faulkner associates the painter's minimalism with the New York school of Glass and Reich; another, on Ellsworth Kelly, discusses Cage's use of chance.

Despite these resonances, the place of music in the book remains somewhat confused. One can find and play the records while at home, but when reading the collection on the train, or at a coffee store, the music is trapped much as ink is on a page. The chasm between forms is deepened by the editor's curious choice to render the playlists in a different font from the remainder of the collection, as if secluding them in their own aesthetic realm. That the poems are 'close' to music comes to imply a distance, as when we tell someone we are 'close' to being in love with them.

If there's anything close to a key for deciphering the collection's set of contradictory fragments, it is a late essay on Val Lewton's 1943 film *The Seventh Victim*. The film is clumsy, and art begins to bleed into reality: characters who are introduced as central are never seen again; a portrait of Dante's Beatrice resembles the main character, but the coincidence is never explored; a doctor played by Tom Conway, the real-life alcoholic, digresses to comment that 'dipsomania can be rather sordid'. This odd exchange, says Ashbery, 'contributes to our sense throughout the film that people are saying anything that comes into their heads, and that the apparent mysteries of the plot are perhaps only a smokescreen for other, ill-defined ones'. One feels the swell of confusions that inhabit Ashbery's own writing: the superimposing of imagination and reality, the demotic vernacular, a mannered prevision infused with the disorientating experience of experiencing things. On which spooky level are we meant to meet him? 'I think one way, perhaps two' he answers in one of the collections final poems; 'it doesn't matter / as long as one can slip by, and easily / into the questioning but not miasmal dark'.

Here I Am

Warsan Shire, *Bless the Daughter Raised by a Voice in Her Head* (Chatto & Windus) £12.99;
Victoria Adukwei Bulley, *Quiet* (Faber) £10.99
Reviewed by Shash Trevett

Much has already been written about this eagerly anticipated debut collection from Warsan Shire. Reviewers have dissected each finely crafted poem, writing about the depiction of violence against women and of the stranglehold of patriarchy in Somali culture. In 'Bless the Qumayo', Shire writes about 'torches of contempt' that 'welcome / us onto this planet'; in fact, the 'cruel person' lurks behind and within the lines of almost every poem in this collection. The cruelty of cultural practices which keep girls 'behind the glass', restricted to watching boys enjoy the freedom of fresh air ('Glitter on the Mouth of Boys'); which cut and mutilate the bodies of girls so that like 'mermaids / with new legs' they 'learn to walk again' ('The Abubakr Girls are Different'); which foam with frenzy at the sight of spilt blood on bridal sheets ('Bless this Blood'); which make 'women flinch at touch'; which form a noose around the necks of young mothers. 'Assimilation' is a masterful dissection of the plight of refugees; 'Bless this House' a milestone in the writing about child abuse. Shire writes with a deliberate urgency, each word

heavy with the undertones of trauma and cultural memory, each poem a cry from the heart for all those women who are subsumed by silence.

And yet... yet, what caught my eye in this collection was the relationship between women themselves. Mothers and daughters featured heavily in Shire's previous publications, and here too women are seen as madonnas, mothers or whores by men, society and, rather subtly, by other women themselves. Women gossip on the phone, 'tallying the sluts of the family', speculating on 'whose hymen fizzes after dark' ('Bless the Qumayo'). The Abubakr girls might walk like mermaids following the ordeal of female genital mutilation, but the horrors are inflicted by women on women who believe that 'daughters are traitors'. The perpetual cycle of violence from grandmother to mother to daughter, absorbed almost unconsciously as all violence often is, can be seen setting root in the next generation. A freshly traumatised Abubakr girl (victim, virginal, not a whore) admonishes the narrator to 'Sit like a girl'. The narrator instead, 'finger[s] the hole in my shorts' and whispers about periods with a younger Abubakr. A quiet rebellion, which signals the hope that at least with the younger sister, Juwariyah, the practice might have reached an end point. In 'Bless Your Ugly Daughter', a young girl, one that 'relatives avoided' is 'forced to gargle rosewater', 'smoked in uunsi', and told that her 'body [is] littered / with ugly things' by the women in the family. In 'Filial Cannibalism' mothers, ordinary mothers,

... feed on the viscid
shame their daughters
are forced to secrete
from glands formed
in the favour of men.

Thus the status quo is maintained: men dictate, women enforce and daughters (before they can even verbalise the concept of freedom) have their wings clipped.

This collection is filled with poems that are angry, strident, accusatory and condemnatory. But Shire also writes tenderness superbly. In 'Bless the Camels' and 'My Father, the Astronaut' a more benign version of masculinity is unpicked. In the former, the relationship between children and their father, naked in all his vulnerability, yet 'held captive' by his 'spinning stories', is laid bare to the light of the 'lonely moon' and the 'hyena's laughter in the wind'. The same moon/Europe/a new life proves unconquerable to 'My Father, the Astronaut', whose hunger drives him towards ultimate failure. A visionary 'who heard the voice of God /... suspended in that dark desert', he is now lost, 'hurtling through space', shielded by angels who allow us occasional glimpses of him by 'drawing back their wings'. 'Midnight in the Foreign Food Aisle' does not refrain from castigating an uncle who, common to most immigrants, makes himself too much at home in the host country. Yet, as time passes, and the women who were 'unable to pronounce [his] name' fade into memory, he is seen in the foreign food aisle of a supermarket ('foreign' to whom?), the smell of turmeric invoking memories that threaten to overwhelm him. The reader is voyeur to this intense moment of vulnerability in a man, now 'totally alone', praying in a 'language [he hasn't] used in years'. The echo of Billie Holiday's 'God Bless this Child' can be heard clearly in this collection full of blessings, (some ironic, some angry, some heartfelt), the best of which, 'Victoria in Illiyin', memorialises the life of Victoria Climbié. In it, 'our Victoria', that child who did not have the chance to 'have her own' is shown receiving all the love, tenderness and care in heaven that she should have received here on earth. 'Gently carried... on the shoulders / of angels, tenderly placed on the upturned palm of God', not one, but '72 devoted mothers' attend to her, wiping (the narrator hopes) away the horror of her memories of life. In spite of what they are subjected to, the girls and women in this collection 'wear / the world well', but the reader is left feeling, along with the poet, that they just didn't have to.

Victoria Adukwei Bulley's much anticipated debut collection doesn't fail to impress. The poems are inventive, deeply thought out, revelling in form and language to communicate ideas with a sense of deliberate urgency. The collection begins authoritatively with 'Declaration', each line ending with a sharply questioning 'if' which slows the reader, making them pause, punctuating the connection between poet and her audience. It is a fantastic start, followed by four poems that deconstruct colonialism with playful authority. Right at the beginning, Adukwei Bulley states that 'you won't find any / lyric shame here', and proceeds to honour and celebrate female Black agency throughout the collection.

In a way, this volume defies easy categorisation. It moves from subject to subject: tender poems about relationships between friends and lovers; about the cycles of birth and death; poems about Ghana, about language and genealogy; poems that celebrate the sheer exuberance of poetry itself. In the title poem 'not quiet as in quiet but' Adukwei Bulley provides us with thirty-one nuanced readings of the word 'quiet'. '[   ] noise' (along with accompanying notes) elevates our understanding of the phenomenon. 'Whose Name Means Honey' is a tender examination of nascent love and 'This Poem', about the poem 'you promised to meet', is a leisurely dissection of the writer's craft. The poems are layered together within the pages but each maintains its separate identity. Reading this collection felt like a meander through an art gallery; each poem displayed static and separate to its neighbour, claiming a place for itself, forcing the reader to stop, to stare and to digest with care.

However, the theme of opposites, binaries, runs all the way through the collection. Accompanying '[   ] noise' is 'black noise': an eye-catching poem of redactions, the heavy black scorings emphasising erasures, questioning the reader 'can you / hear me? can you / see me / now?'. 'The Ultra-Black Fish', with its pseudo-scientific language in which the deep-sea fish 'became a living black hole', is a companion piece to 'towards a black mirror' (part of the 'fabula' sequence). In the latter Adukwei Bulley draws on Black Feminist theory to examine our need (as a society, as a culture) for opposites. The collection ends where it began, back with the colonial imperative to classify, to revel in the othering of encounters so that it can always be found 'on the victorious team of a series of / binaries'. In order for [   ] noise to be understood, black noise

needs to be silenced; in order for white bodies to be seen fully, the black body needs to be set up in opposition. Yet here, Adukwei Bulley sets about laying claim to the black mirror, which absorbs but refuses to be used as a reflector: in it,

dark & potent as space itself. she looks, she sees & pleased, then, she
says: *there now, see, here I am.*

Five First Collections

Jake Morris-Campbell, *Corrigenda for Costafine Town* (Blue Diode) £10
Joanna Nissel, *Guerrilla Brightenings* (Against the Grain) £6
Tristan Moss, *The Cold War* (Lapwing) £10
Chaucer Cameron, *In an Ideal World I'd Not Be Murdered* (Against the Grain) £6
M Stasiak, *Enchant / Extinguish* (Shearsman) £6.50
Reviewed by Ian Seed

Jake Morris-Campbell's first full-length collection, *Corrigenda for Costafine Town,* navigates between the working-class world he grew up in and the culturally middle-class one he now inhabits. With an insightful, wry lyricism, Morris-Campbell investigates the history and geography of North-East landscapes, cityscapes and seascapes, how they tie in with his own family, and the ways in which the usage of different types of language creates different perspectives and realities. The question of identity is rendered more complex by the fact that the region itself has been irreparably altered over the past two decades or so by the forces of globalisation, which in turn has split families politically, noticeably over attitudes towards Europe, though deeper bonds can prevail:

I could tell by the way he clasped the cup
how much he really needed a fag
that I should focus on the sea
not mention politics or family
or the politics of families
so that as long as nothing was said
we could concentrate solely
the way men do
on the scrunch of sand
between his children's toes
('Grapnel')

Within this context, the poet, as the Homeric 'wanderer returned', sometimes feels like an imposter, yet through his writing seeks to discover an authentic vision of the self rooted, if not always in place and time, then in the changing realities of the world we live in.

Joanna Nissel's chapbook, *Guerrilla Brightenings*, is a navigation of the selves of past and present. Taken together the poems represent a coming-of-age. Landscape is crucial here, in this case the streets, gardens and beaches of Brighton, which are lent an extra layer of defamiliarisation by the fact that many of the poems are set during the Covid lockdown. This offers the space for deeper reflection and more nuanced observation, conveyed with unsentimental tenderness and gentle humour: 'Behind hedgerows, / I hear a woman tell her child // to stop flicking beetles from the magnolia' (from 'On rediscovering a favourite dress, May 2020').

There are two hilarious and oddly disturbing found poems taken from snippets of social media: 'In lieu of / privileged little cunts / lord bless some of the real ones / the nice weather / a cup of tea' (from 'Meantime'). At the same time, Nissel is capable of writing poignantly of loss: 'don't look out to the sea's heat-hazed horizon / don't notice the gulls calling you home' (from 'visit from my unborn child').

In a series of deceptively simple poems, Tristan Moss's chapbook, *The Cold War*, examines the self in terms of family relationships, often seen within the political context of the Cold War; his mother and father were political activists in the Seventies and early Eighties. Taken together, the poems read as an elegy both for his mother, who died in 2021, and for his father, who died in 1990 in a motorway accident. The imagery catches us by surprise, as the poems unfold in stripped down yet evocative narratives, which linger in the mind after reading:

But for today, I think back
to when there were fields,
open skies and a farm,
where my father looked up
from chopping wood
and smiled at me.
('A Space in the Trees')

In an Ideal World I'd Not Be Murdered is in many respects a poetry of the destruction of the self, exploring the impact of prostitution. Chaucer Cameron writes out of her own experience and those of people she has known. The poems are direct, sparsely written, and often read like short documentary films (she is a filmmaker as well as a poet). There is a powerful and harrowing lyric at work here. Cameron refuses to embellish or eroticise. Wisely, she does not explicitly take a moral stance or condemn the 'clients', but instead shows us the psychological and social effects of leading a life where a woman 'chooses' to have sex with people she doesn't want to have sex with, and is continually exposed to the threat of serious violence. One coping mechanism is to escape mentally into another world. There can be a dark humour to this, as in this excerpt from the ironically songlike 'Cartoons' (which uses slashes to create an extra staccato effect):

It's funny what you think of/ when you're gagging/ for your life
when you hear the car doors/ click/
when the music is turned up/ and you put on your disguise.

Tonight/ it was The Flintstones/ I watched them as a kid/

M Stasiak's *Enchant / Extinguish* recalls to mind Sylvia Plath's *Ariel* in its attention to craft, its heightened use of language, and its use of a quasi-surreal imagery in response to situations which may seem ordinary, but which can be terrifying in the way they may lead to a collapse of one's sense of identity, or which represent a longing to escape an identity one feels trapped in:

When you stretched the blanket over me
& somehow I thought of corpses
laid out in drawers in some mortuary someplace
although I was in our living room & only
almost-asleep, it held me down,
and I was a fly buzzing against steel mesh
& outside was a room and inside
was the whole of everything & I was
the mesh and the buzz as well as the fly
(From 'Buzzing')

The poems come together as a kind of geology of the self, relating personal identity to wider issues of society and ecology, revealing ways in which we avoid genuine relationships both with others and our environment. They ask how we might, however impossible it may seem, achieve a deeper authenticity in the world we live in.

Contributor Notes

Antony Huen is an academic from Hong Kong. He has published poems in *amberflora, Dark Horse, harana poetry, Ink, Sweat & Tears and Poetry Wales*, and articles in *Compass, New Defences of Poetry, The Oxonian Review, Wasafiri and World Literature Today.* He is the winner of the inaugural *Wasafiri* Essay Prize. Born in Colorado, **Julith Jedamus** has lived in London for twenty-five years. A poet and novelist, she edits books about nature and the environment. **Rebecca Watts** is the author of two poetry collections, *The Met Office Advises Caution* (2016) and *Red Gloves* (2020), and editor of *Elizabeth Jennings: New Selected Poems* (2019), all published by Carcanet. **Ian Seed**'s recent collections include *New York Hotel* (Shearsman, 2018), selected by Mark Ford as *TLS Book of the Year*, and *The Underground Cabaret* (Shearsman, 2020). His translations include *The Thief of Talant* (Wakefield 2016), the first translation into English from the French of Pierre Reverdy's *Le voleur de Talan*, and *The Dice Cup* (Wakefield, 2022), from the French of Max Jacob's *Le Cornet à dés*. **Harry Sanderson** teaches law to undergraduates at Sidney Sussex College, Cambridge. **Tony Roberts** is the author of five collections of poetry and two books of essays on poets and critics for Shoestring Press, most recently *The Taste of My Mornings* (2019). He is currently completing a third. **Clara Dawson** is a Senior Lecturer in Victorian Literature at the University of Manchester. Her research in nineteenth-century poetry spans print culture and environmental humanities. **Oksana Maksymchuk** is the author of the poetry collections *Xenia* and *Lovy* in the Ukrainian. Her English-language poems appeared in *AGNI, Irish Times, Paris Review* and *Poetry Review*. **Jodie Hollander**'s work has appeared in journals such as *Poetry Review, Yale Review, PN Review, Kenyon Review, Poetry London, Hudson Review, Dark Horse, The New Criterion, Rialto, Verse Daily, Best Australian Poems of 2011*, and *Best Australian Poems of 2015.* Her debut full-length collection, *My Dark Horses*, was published with Liverpool University Press & Oxford University Press. Her second collection,

Nocturne, will be published with the Liverpool & Oxford University Press in the spring of 2023. She currently lives in Fort Collins, Colorado. **Craig Raine** is a poet, novelist, literary critic and dramatist. He was the editor of *Areté* from 1999 to 2019. His last book was *My Grandmother's Glass Eye: A Look at Poetry* (2019). He is an Emeritus Fellow of New College, Oxford. **Joseph Minden** is a poet and secondary school teacher. His first collection, *Poppy*, is out with Carcanet in November. **Joe Carrick-Varty** is a British-Irish poet, writer and founding editor of *bath magg*. His debut book of poems, *More Sky*, is forthcoming with Carcanet in Januaury 2023. **Antony Huen** is a critic and academic. His essay on the 'Hong Kong School' of poets won the inaugural Wasafiri Essay Prize. He also writes poems and has published in *Dark Horse* and *Poetry Wales*. **Stanley Moss**, ninety-seven years young, has just published *Always Alwaysland* in the US with 7 Stories/Random House. In the UK, he's published ten books with Carcanet/Anvil, most recently *God Breaketh Not All Men's Hearts Alike, Poems 1948–2019.* **Alexandra Corrin-Tachibana**'s debut collection *Sing me down from the dark* was published by Salt in October 2022. Her most recent work is soon to be published in *The Moth*. **Robert Griffiths** has published essays and poetry in magazines (*Acumen, Philosophy Now, The Spectator, Rialto*). He is writing a book entitled *God and the Philosophers*. **Horatio Morpurgo** writes on the environment, history and European Affairs for many publications. He organised the campaign to commemorate Stefan Zweig's residence in London. *The Paradoxal Compass* (Notting Hill Editions, 2017) argues for the continuing relevance of early modern history to today's environmental movement. An earlier essay about Berdychiv, central Ukraine, 'Tunnels Under Ukraine', featured in *Afterwardsness* (Erewhon, 2022). **Audrey Henderson**'s collection *Airstream* was shortlisted for the Saltire Society First Book award. Originally from Edinburgh and now living in Boston, she was a Hawthornden Fellow.

Editors
Michael Schmidt
John McAuliffe

Editorial Manager
Andrew Latimer

Contributing Editors
Vahni Capildeo
Sasha Dugdale
Will Harris

Proofreader
Maren Meinhardt

Designer
Andrew Latimer

Editorial address
The Editors at the address on the right. Manuscripts cannot be returned unless accompanied by a stamped addressed envelope or international reply coupon.

Trade distributors
NBN International

Represented by
Compass IPS Ltd

Copyright
© 2022 Poetry Nation Review
All rights reserved
ISBN 978-1-80017-287-6
ISBN 0144-7076

Subscriptions—6 issues
  INDIVIDUAL–print and digital:
£45; abroad £65
  INSTITUTIONS–print only:
  £76; abroad £90
  INSTITUTIONS–digital only:
  from Exact Editions (https://shop.exacteditions.com/gb/pn-review) to: PN Review, Alliance House, 30 Cross Street, Manchester, M2 7AQ, UK.

Supported by

Supported using public funding by
ARTS COUNCIL ENGLAND